Young Architects 21
Just

Young Architects 21
Just

Acknowledgments by
Paul Lewis
Foreword by
Mario Gooden
Introduction by
Anne Rieselbach

Rachel G. Barnard
Young New Yorkers

Jennifer Bonner
MALL

**Virginia Black,
Rosana Elkhatib, and
Gabrielle Printz**
feminist architecture
collaborative

Mira Hasson Henry
(HA)

Gregory Melitonov
Taller KEN

Cyrus Peñarroyo
EXTENTS

The Architectural
League of New York

Co-published by
The Architectural League of New York
and ORO Editions

The Architectural League of New York
594 Broadway, Suite 607
New York, NY 10012
www.archleague.org

ORO Editions
www.oroeditions.com

To read interviews with each firm,
please visit archleague.org.

Editor Anne Rieselbach
Managing Editor Catarina Flaksman
Consulting Editor Andrea Monfried
Cover Design Pentagram / Jena Sher
Interior Layout Jena Sher Graphic Design

This publication is supported, in part, by
public funds from the New York City
Department of Cultural Affairs in partnership
with the City Council.

We thank ORO Editions for their generous
contribution to this publication.

The 2019 League Prize program was
also made possible by Elise Jaffe + Jeffrey
Brown, Hunter Douglas Architectural,
Rachel Judlowe, Elizabeth Kubany, and
Tischler und Sohn.

Installation photos at Parsons School
of Design at The New School
© David Sundberg/Esto

Library of Congress Control Number:
2021913141
ISBN 978-1-954081-10-9

Contents

7 **Acknowledgments**
Paul Lewis

8 **Foreword**
Mario Gooden

11 **Introduction**
Anne Rieselbach

16 **Biographies**

20 **Rachel G. Barnard**
Young New Yorkers

44 **Jennifer Bonner**
MALL

70 **Virginia Black,
Rosana Elkhatib, and
Gabrielle Printz**
feminist architecture
collaborative

98 **Mira Hasson Henry**
(HA)

122 **Gregory Melitonov**
Taller KEN

148 **Cyrus Peñarroyo**
EXTENTS

Acknowledgments

Paul Lewis

President, The Architectural League of New York

One of the distinguishing criteria of The Architectural League Prize for Young Architects + Designers is that entrants must be ten years or less out of a bachelor's or master's degree program. This span is a fascinating and fruitful period in a designer's evolution, a period characterized by tension between evoking and transcending the defining characteristics of previous education and mentorship. Marked with clairvoyance, the selection of the theme *just*—by League Prize Committee Isabel Abascal, Bryony Roberts, and Anya Sirota—catalyzed a sense of urgency about social and racial equity, which is fundamental to the winning architects and designers. The theme elevates and foregrounds the work, which is mature beyond its years.

Competition jurors Mario Gooden, Juliet Kinchin, and I were impressed by the idiosyncratic character and the playful seriousness of each of the winners. We offer our thanks and gratitude to League program director Anne Rieselbach, who has once again crafted a process that enables younger talent to thrive and receive deserved public attention. This recognition takes many forms, including the competition, an exhibition, digital programming, lectures, and this book, which Anne and League program manager Catarina Flaksman painstakingly guide to fruition. Pentagram was instrumental in the development of the competition and exhibition graphics, and David Sundberg/Esto photographed the installation with his usual eloquence. This publication would not be possible without the dedication of consulting editor Andrea Monfried and graphic designer Jena Sher.

We are grateful to Elise Jaffe + Jeffrey Brown, Hunter Douglas Architectural, Rachel Judlowe, Elizabeth Kubany, and Tischler und Sohn for their support of the League Prize. The program is also supported by the Next Generation and J. Clawson Mills Funds of The Architectural League. We acknowledge additional support for this publication by public funds from the New York City Department of Cultural Affairs in partnership with the City Council. We thank ORO Editions for both publishing and sponsoring this volume.

The exhibition and lecture series were cosponsored and hosted by the Sheila C. Johnson Design Center, Parsons School of Design at The New School. The League thanks the School of Constructed Environments at Parsons School of Design at The New School for additional support.

Foreword
Mario Gooden
Juror; Founding Principal, Huff + Gooden Architects

Spatial Justice/Spatial Practice

Upon reflection, the theme of the 2019 League Prize—*just*—can be considered in different ways in an architectural work, including formally, materially, contextually, and culturally. The competition brief offered a series of thought-provoking questions, among them:

> How might architecture serve justice? Confront complex challenges across scales, mediums, and geographies? Build new equitable paradigms for action? Can architecture engage a breadth of constituencies, environments, and species? In an era of global turbulence, how might architecture's ends justify the means? Can architects advocate for architectural excellence and beauty while still addressing social concerns? Can just architecture, with its laborious process from conceptualization to construction, become a justified statement in itself?

In the wake of the summer of 2020 and the convergence of the COVID-19 pandemic; the Black Lives Matter movement and its intersectionality with Black Trans Lives and Say Her Name; and the intensifying need for a global response to climate change and environmental justice, it is clear that "just" is not merely an idea, option, or question for architecture but an urgent necessity. Amid calls to decolonize architectural pedagogies, unlearn Whiteness in the academy and in the profession, and address the social inequities of climate change and environmental degradation, questions of "just" and justice are in fact questions of space (both conceptual and theoretical) and space making that are central to the purview of architecture.

Writing in *Architecture as Space*, Italian architect, historian, and curator Bruno Zevi identifies space as both subject and object of architecture. Oscillating between these two positions in conceiving and representing architectural space dislodges the primacy of the ideal Vitruvian subject (historically rendered as European, White, male, and able-bodied) as the origin and master of a universal worldview, thus creating an epistemic rupture that gives way to discursive spaces such as social, cultural, and political spaces as well as spaces of enclosure. Zevi goes on to explain that the experience of space is not limited to the formal properties of the architectural object but extends to the city, to the streets, squares, alleys, parks, playgrounds, gardens, and other spaces where humans have defined a void, thus creating an enclosure. But what are the implications of enclosure with regards to interior versus exterior; inside versus outside; exclusive versus inclusive; sameness versus alterity?

John Locke associates enclosure with land possession and property rights in his *Second Treatise of Civil Government*. For Locke, labor provides the ultimate basis for legitimate property rights. In colonial contexts, the labor of the settler—to improve, till, cultivate, or produce plants or animals on the land—provided the right to enclosure and to colonial property formation. For in the British imperial overseas colonies of North America, Africa, India, and New Zealand, there was no precolonial law governing these lands that established a *commons* (land or resources belonging to or affecting the whole of a community) of universal scope corresponding with nature itself.

In the treatise, there are repeated references to the poverty of "commoners" (that is, Indigenous peoples) and to the superiority of enclosures. Allen Greer of McGill University notes that Locke consistently links the words "commons," "waste," "commoner," "Indian," "America," and "poverty" in negative contexts.[1] Furthermore, Locke writes, "For I ask, whether in the wild woods and uncultivated waste of *America*, left to nature, without any improvement, tillage or husbandry, a thousand acres yield the needy and wretched inhabitants as many conveniencies of life, as ten acres of equally fertile land do in *Devonshire*, where they are well cultivated?"[2] Thus the lands in North America and other overseas colonies were available for colonial enclosure and possession and, by extension, for Indigenous dispossession. This history directly implicates the plantation and its present-day mechanisms of exploitation—the reservation, the ghetto, the prison, and the redlined neighborhood— as sites of enclosure and subjugation. In the United States, the COVID-19 pandemic reified these enclosures, with the populations most affected by the virus as well as the greatest concentrations of laborers deemed "essential workers" residing in redlined neighborhoods. Thus these enclosures delineate the boundaries between life and death as the spatial consequences of persistent social and racial inequalities. Hence, the urgent necessity of "just" must answer above all to questions of *spatial justice*.

1 Allen Greer, "Commons and Enclosure in the Colonization of North America," *American Historical Review* 117, no. 2 (April 2012): 367.
2 John Locke, "Of Property," *Two Treatises of Government* (1689), §37.

An emphasis on spatial justice requires, first, an examination of the inseparability between the spatial and the social. Spatial justice also involves consideration of the fair and equitable distribution in space of socially valued resources such as land, urban space, and, more broadly, the environment. Second, spatial justice requires the examination of both process and outcome, with social processes shaping space and spatiality shaping social processes. While underscoring spatial justice does not displace other considerations of "just," it may provide a means to dismantle or at least reverse the biases that cast questions of spatial justice in the realm of benevolence and paternalism on the part of the architect. Thus, the 2019 League Prize prompt can now be read through a clearer lens and not only in hindsight.

A critical spatial analysis of the multidisciplinary works created by the Prize winners reveals questions regarding the nature of enclosures, social, political, or cultural, and questions regarding socio-material processes. Whether explicitly corporeal or carceral, or obsessively conditioned by representational modalities, the works ultimately release their gaze from the architectural object in favor of understanding "just" in the intersecting contexts of space, knowledge, and power. In a 1982 interview published in the architectural journal *Skyline*, French philosopher Michel Foucault describes how the Industrial Revolution brought about profound changes in the understanding and delineation of space. With space no longer reserved for the control of territory and governing people within it, fundamental spatial relationships emerged from the exercise of power and territory as well as from social transformations that developed through new technologies and economic processes. In the American colonies, this intersection of space and power coincided with the racialization of space in which the enactment of slave codes restricted the movements and gatherings of enslaved Africans. Foucault states that it is not possible to say that a thing is of the order of either liberation or oppression; instead, he concedes that architectural projects are complicit in reshaping the public sphere as simultaneous forces of liberation and forces of resistance. The problem of space, Foucault emphasizes, is that "liberty is a practice" and that, in the face of systemic oppression, liberatory practices, spatial and otherwise, remain possible.[3] This axiom exposes the spatial causality of just/injust and also the embedding, in space and in multiscalar geographies, of justice/injustice—from the body and the corporeal through the city and nation-states and to the global scale.

3 Michel Foucault, "Space, Knowledge, and Power," interview by Paul Rabinow, *Skyline*, March 1982, in *The Foucault Reader* (New York: Pantheon, 1984), 245.

Introduction
Anne Rieselbach
Program Director, The Architectural League of New York

The 2019 Architectural League Prize committee asked competition entrants to consider the *just* in how they approach the practice of architecture, whether through experimentation in research and design advocacy or by advancing speculative and applied techniques. The competition winners' interpretations of *just* ranged in scale from reimagining urban institutions to reevaluating domestic spaces to rethinking the implications of the term in relation to the female body. The installations for the League's annual exhibition in the galleries of Parsons School of Design at The New School continued to investigate the competition theme via contemporary social issues, including criminal justice reform, public space, and digital culture.

Young New Yorkers founder and executive director Rachel G. Barnard fabricated an abstract solitary confinement cell in the galleries. The compressed carceral space—eight by six feet with vibrant pink bungee cord "bars"—incorporated suspended headphones playing young people's accounts of confinement. These teenagers and young adults were diverted to YNY's design-based restorative justice programs rather than sentenced to jail. Barnard chose a multisensory approach to highlight participants' lived experiences: in 2011, when she founded the program, the city held an average of a hundred teens in solitary confinement at any given time. The installation, says Barnard, asked visitors "to engage directly with the young people's stories and hear their reflections on what it could be like if New York City were indeed just."

Jennifer Bonner's installation centered on her firm MALL's design for Haus Gables in Atlanta, Georgia. When it was built in 2018, the house was one of a handful of single-family residences in the United States constructed primarily of cross-laminated timber. Large photographs of the house provided a backdrop for two study models perched atop finished wooden art crates and pallets: *The Dollhaus*, a 1:12 scale model of Haus Gables with selected interior finishes, and *Glittery Faux-Facade*, a facade mock-up made of stucco with a dash finish of reflective glass beads. Bonner also stacked a set of her *Domestic Hats* study models of irregular roof massing along-side the two pieces, evidencing her self-described "obsession with domestic roof typologies." The wry title of her competition portfolio—"just roofs"—referred to the same fascination.

feminist architecture collaborative partners Virginia Black, Gabrielle Printz, and Rosana Elkhatib displayed a partial replica of *Cosmo-Clinical Interiors of Beirut*, an installation first exhibited at Vi Per gallery in Prague. The designers described their full-scale clinic assemblage as drawing on the "decorated spaces of bodily reconstruction in Lebanon's destination city for hymenoplastic and other cosmetic procedures." A curtained exam cubicle, complete with self-examination chair (transparent inflatable seat over curved mirror) and VR viewer ("a room you can wear"), offered an "intimate look at the aesthetic practices that shape the body and the choices women make through desire or duress." The project is part of f-architecture's broader study of the cultural and physical construction of virginity in the Middle East and North Africa and the "procedures by which the body itself is designed."

Four themes—mining tradition, reflecting context, shaping culture, and restoring community—linked four design-build projects by Taller KEN. Documentary drawings and photographs illustrated the studio's approach to the public realm. Taller KEN principal (and cofounder, with Inés Guzmán) Gregory Melitonov said the office "strives for an architecture with broad appeal" while working alongside local communities. The four projects included a temporary multiuse pavilion, a café and event space, and a plan to rehabilitate a disused rail depot, all in Guatemala City, and a community school in Roluos, Cambodia. The graphic material was arrayed on a field of colorful vinyl stripes—a full-scale mock-up for a fifth project, a multiyear public art installation in downtown Brooklyn.

Mira Hasson Henry's photographs and models documented *Rough Coat*, a 2018 installation at SCI-Arc Gallery, and Silver House Studio, a building proposal designed in collaboration with Matthew Au. *Rough Coat* transformed the exhibition space into an interior landscape centered on a facade-scale blanket and two large beds. The components explored a tactile building system, exploiting the use of pliable stucco to render the familiar strange. Silver House Studio advanced the tectonic and aesthetic qualities of *Rough Coat* in an artist's studio in Los Angeles. A model built up of layers of materials—roof cladding, frame, and interior insulation hung over an internal frame— demonstrated how the studio interacts with the adjacent residence, painted silver by the client. The lap siding of the existing building, translated into a layer of quilted insulation for the studio, contributed to this subtle defamiliarization of a typical bungalow.

Tiered levels of a lavender, foam-padded, off-the-shelf data floor system supported what Cyrus Peñarroyo described as the "physical stuff of media." Screens, tethered by a tangle of coiled extension cords, displayed projects by EXTENTS, the design collaborative founded by Peñarroyo (with McLain Clutter). These "platforms on platforms" rested on custom-milled low-density fiberboard and high-density foam padding embossed with abstract delineations from architectural drawing software. On top of the platforms were screens presenting images and videos of the firm's work. Foam cylinders provided seating, allowing visitors to engage with the work of all six winning firms. According to Peñarroyo, the interactive installation encouraged "onlookers to question their media viewing habits and to draw relationships between all the work featured in the gallery."

As Mario Gooden observes in the foreword to this publication, the theme, conceived by League Prize committee members Isabel Abascal, Bryony Roberts, and Anya Sirota, was prescient, given the events of 2020. The committee observed that "escalating conditions of sociopolitical turmoil and environmental calamity have prompted renewed attention to the ethics of architecture" (a statement that only begins to describe the challenges facing the profession). Yet the winners' unwavering commitment to innovation through design provides productive means to address what the committee described as "the implicit tensions between architecture's affinity for the 'just so' in materials, tectonics, and organization, and a call to act justly."

Biographies

Rachel G. Barnard / Young New Yorkers
New York, New York

Rachel G. Barnard is a social practice artist trained as an architect. She is the NYC Public Artist in Residence with the Department of Probation and a fellow at A Blade of Grass. She holds an MS in advanced architectural design from the Columbia University Graduate School of Architecture, Planning and Preservation in New York and a BArch from the University of Queensland in Australia.

Barnard established Young New Yorkers in 2011 with a mission to use art to transform the criminal legal system. Since its founding, more than 1,300 young people (between 14 and 25 years old) have been ordered to make art in YNY programs rather than sentenced to jail time or other sanctions. YNY culminates in a participant-led public art project that addresses a criminal legal issue; the young people invite judges and other court professionals to the exhibition, humanizing the culture of the courtroom.

Barnard is responsible for YNY's creative direction, program development, and fundraising. She guided the collaborative development of YNY's programs and initiated sustainable partnerships with key criminal legal partners.

Jennifer Bonner / MALL
Boston, Massachusetts

Born in Alabama, Jennifer Bonner founded MALL in 2009 as a creative practice for art and architecture. MALL—Mass Architectural Loopty Loops or Maximum Arches with Limited Liability—is an acronym with built-in flexibility. Bonner's work often involves projects that hack typologies, take creative risks, reference popular culture, and invent representation.

MALL's projects have been published in magazines and journals including *Architect*, *Metropolis*, *Azure*, *Wallpaper*, *Flat Out*, *PLAT*, *Offramp, Log*, and *MAS Context*. Bonner is the co-editor of *Blank: Speculations on CLT*, author of *A Guide to the Dirty South: Atlanta*, editor of *Platform: Still Life*, and guest editor for an *Art Papers* special issue on the architecture and design of Los Angeles. Her work has been exhibited at the Istanbul Design Biennial, Chicago Architecture Biennial, Design Biennial Boston, Yve Yang Gallery, and pinkcomma gallery. In 2021, she was awarded the United States Artists Fellowship in Architecture.

Bonner holds a BArch from Auburn University in Alabama, where she attended the Rural Studio, and an MArch from the Harvard University Graduate School of Design in Cambridge. She is an associate professor of architecture at Harvard GSD.

Virginia Black, Rosana Elkhatib, and Gabrielle Printz /
feminist architecture collaborative
Brooklyn, New York

feminist architecture collaborative is a three-woman architectural research enterprise initiated in 2016 by Virginia Black, Rosana Elkhatib, and Gabrielle Printz. f-architecture is a vehicle for work aimed at disentangling the contemporary spatial politics of bodies, both intimately and globally. The practitioners produce research and public outcomes across theoretical and material registers, locating new forms of architectural work by means of critical relationships with collaborators in Amazonian Ecuador, Jordan, and New York. f-architecture is a former member of the NEW INC incubator, where the collaborators pitched a start-up for synthetic hymen manufacture as a cover for other critical projects.

Black, Elkhatib, and Printz found each other at Columbia University Graduate School of Architecture, Planning and Preservation in New York, where each earned an MS in critical, curatorial, and conceptual practices in architecture. Virginia Black holds an MArch from the University of Michigan A. Alfred Taubman College of Architecture and Urban Planning in Ann Arbor and a BA in architecture from Clemson University in South Carolina. Rosana Elkhatib holds a BArch from the Illinois Institute of Technology in Chicago. Gabrielle Printz is a PhD candidate at the Yale School of Architecture in New Haven. She has an MArch from the University of Buffalo School of Architecture and Planning and a BA in political science and art history from Canisius College in Buffalo. The three maintain their practice and friendship in Brooklyn, New York.

Mira Hasson Henry / (HA)
Los Angeles, California

Mira Hasson Henry is a designer and educator. She is the principal of (HA) and the co-principal of the collaborative practice Current Interests. Henry's built work is grounded in notions of material specificity, color relationships, and assembly details as well as in an engagement with critical cultural thinking.

Henry holds a BA in art history from the University of Chicago and an MArch from UCLA School of the Arts and Architecture. She has received the Henry Adams Medal from the AIA and the Archiprix International Gold Medal. Her research and writing focus on architecture, race, and materiality and have been published in journals including *Harvard Design Magazine, Log,* and *Pidgin.* She is on the faculty at Southern California Institute for Architecture in Los Angeles and has held visiting faculty positions at Princeton University and Harvard University Graduate School of Design. Prior to teaching and starting her own office, Henry worked as a lead designer for Talbot McLanahan Architect, Venice, California; Office dA, Boston; and Monica Ponce de Leon Studio, New York.

Gregory Melitonov / Taller KEN
New York, New York / Guatemala City, Guatemala

Taller KEN focuses on playful design with social and cultural relevance. Founded by Gregory Melitonov and Inés Guzmán in 2013, the practice embraces the collaborative nature of partnerships. Incorporating numerous voices, Taller KEN's work goes beyond elevating elements of design to create an architecture with broad appeal.

The firm often works in developing countries and urban areas defined by unbalanced growth and social inequity. Realizing projects in this context has helped the practice establish its approach to working in the public realm. In 2016, Taller KEN began an annual design-build initiative, FUNdaMENTAL, to work more closely with local communities. The program brings design interns together with real-world problems and partners to create public urban interventions that benefit the collective good.

Before founding Taller KEN, Melitonov worked for Renzo Piano Building Workshop as part of the design team for the Whitney Museum of American Art and the headquarters for the High Line, both in New York. Melitonov holds an MArch from Yale School of Architecture in New Haven and a BS in studio art from Skidmore College in Saratoga Springs.

Cyrus Peñarroyo / EXTENTS
Ann Arbor, Michigan

Cyrus Peñarroyo founded EXTENTS in 2017 with McLain Clutter. The collaborative examines the interrelationship between media and built environments. Central to the practice is a commitment to architecture's role as a medium of public life, progressive culture, and common sense. Their work cultivates unconventional approaches to collectivity, excess, and tectonic assembly in order to suggest other ways of being in the world. EXTENTS has exhibited projects at Materials & Applications in Los Angeles, pinkcomma gallery in Boston, The New School in New York, Princeton University School of Architecture, and Harvard University Graduate School of Design.

Peñarroyo received an MArch from Princeton University and a BS in architecture from the University of Illinois at Chicago. He is an assistant professor at the University of Michigan A. Alfred Taubman College of Architecture and Urban Planning in Ann Arbor, where he was the 2015–2016 William Muschenheim Fellow. His research studies the influence of networked technologies on urbanization.

Rachel G. Barnard

Young New Yorkers

22 *UNITY: Visions for Neighborhood Policing*
24 *Get Your Thrive On!*
28 *Courtroom Spectacular!*
32 *Wisdom Gift Exchange*
36 *Artist Advocates*
40 *Wisdom Pavilion*

Young New Yorkers, established by Rachel G. Barnard in 2011, uses art and design to bring systemic change to the ways in which teens and young adults are arrested, prosecuted, and sentenced in New York City. This effort is centered on YNY's Restorative Arts Diversion Program, which allows young people to avoid jail and exit the criminal legal system promptly. In this way, young adults do not incur a record, the consequences of which can be devastating, among them restricted access to education, employment, housing, and other social services. Since 2012, more than 1,300 young people have been diverted from the system through YNY activities.

RAD programs range in length from one day to eight weeks. They are intended to be in proportion to the charges against the young people, though the specifics are generally at the discretion of the prosecutors. Each series has between four and twelve participants and is facilitated by a diverse team that includes at least one previous RAD graduate. The first portion of the programs focuses on restorative arts practices that allow young adults to address the impact of their actions, explore the systematic injustices of the legal system, and create positive self-narratives for the future. In the second half of each program, young people become artist-advocates for themselves and for a reformed criminal legal system.

One component of RAD is designing and hosting interactive courtroom exhibitions that advocate for change around a specific issue of criminal justice. Teens and young adults invite the court professionals involved in their charges and sentencing to attend. Bringing young people and criminal legal actors together in this context humanizes the culture of the courtroom. This experience leads to a transformed ethos among courtroom professionals, one in which they can use their considerable discretionary power to offer better outcomes to young adults who have been arrested, including dismissing and sealing their cases.

Barnard's original proposal for YNY put forward a public art project that would allow 16- and 17-year-olds who were being prosecuted as adults in New York to advocate for change. However, in early 2012, Jonathan Lippman, former chief judge of New York State, announced a campaign to "Raise the Age" of criminal responsibility from 16 to 18. In response, Barnard recast YNY as the first arts-based alternative to incarceration. Joseph E. Gubbay, a judge in New York City Criminal Courts in Kings County, adopted the initiative, and in August 2012, YNY conducted its first eight-week RAD program. The eight young men who completed the inaugural sessions had their cases dismissed and sealed.

UNITY: *Visions for Neighborhood Policing*
Eastern District Court

New York, New York, summer 2017

The participants in this eight-week RAD program repeatedly shared their traumas with police brutality, and so they chose excessive police force as the focus of their courtroom exhibition. The young people imagined local communities and police forces that did not stand in violent opposition. The art project invited attendees—friends, family, judges, prosecutors, and police—to describe visions for neighborhood policing that centered on first acknowledging the generational harm of unjust policing practices on communities of color and then stepping toward accountability on both sides. Each guest was invited to write down insights on the past and visions for the future. The notes were tied to a sculpture that spelled the word *unity* with purple roses. In exchange for their wisdom, the graduating YNY participants gifted each attendee a rose from the Unity sculpture.

   The installation allowed for open interactions between the YNY graduates and the police officers. This new dynamic between traditionally conflicting groups encouraged meaningful dialogues about past harm and what it may take to create a peaceful and unified future.

opposite, top:
YNY graduates and
community in front
of the Unity sculpture

opposite, bottom:
YNY participant
giving Judge Joseph
E. Gubbay a rose
in exchange for his
vision of policing
Photos: Mansura Khanam

Get Your Thrive On!
Eastern District Court
New York, New York, winter 2018

Disparities in the application of justice were the subject of this RAD program. While some teens and young adults avoid arrest or are excused from prosecution and given a chance to learn from their mistakes, others—primarily Black and Brown and generally from low-income neighborhoods—are criminalized for identical infractions. Once in the court system, this group faces collateral consequences such as narrowed access to housing, education, and employment.

The exhibition that resulted from the eight-week program, *Get Your Thrive On!*, turned the courtroom into a game show. Five obelisks contained suspended discs that posed a series of questions on what is required to advance from surviving to thriving, to meet all of a person's needs, be they physical, emotional, or in service of realizing potential. Maslow's hierarchy of needs—physiological needs, safety, love and belonging, esteem, and self-actualization—informed this deliberation. Attendees applied stickers to the discs to identify whether they had ever gone hungry, not had a place to sleep, or felt unsafe in their daily lives. The exercise, disguised as a playful Q&A, revealed to the guests the difficulties faced by some YNY participants in simply meeting basic needs.

Each obelisk was associated with a game station corresponding to one of Maslow's needs. The fifth station addressed self-actualization, that is, the need for creativity, growth, and achieving a person's full potential. By satisfying needs in the other four categories, participants, guests, and criminal legal partners had cleared the way to focus on identifying their aspirations. Attendees recorded their dreams as well as how those dreams would contribute to the community and to a better world. The visions were added to a mobile of community aspirations. Photographs documented the attendees as they stood, supported by the larger community, in the power of their full potential.

opposite: NYC Assistant District Attorney Christine Payne responding to questions based on Maslow's hierarchy of needs Photo: Mansura Khanam

top, left: Saadiq Newton Boyd of Brooklyn Justice Initiatives responding to questions based on Maslow's hierarchy of needs

top, right: Kristine Herman, director of policy at Brooklyn Defender Services, attaching her dreams to the community aspirations mobile

bottom: YNY graduate/peer mentor Shawnti and court security officer shaking hands

Photos: Mansura Khanam

Courtroom Spectacular!
Eastern District Court
New York, New York, spring 2018

Long-established neuroscience asserts that young people don't fully develop consequential thinking—wise and informed decision making—until the age of 25. This group of RAD participants was concerned about teens and young people being prosecuted as adults given that, scientifically, they had adolescent brains and were still maturing. In *Courtroom Spectacular!*, the resulting installation, YNY participants imagined a judicial space that, instead of wielding punitive sanctions, promotes magnificent futures for young adults, their communities, and their beloved New York City.

Guests learned some of the science behind brain development, identifying whether their own brains were those of a child, adolescent, adult, or senior. Then the attendees took the Brainiac Quiz, developed by the YNY participants. Questions asked for the age at which the New York criminal legal system considers a teenager to be an adult (at the time, it was 16), the age at which neuroscience regards an individual as possessing fully developed consequential thinking (25), the duration of a criminal record (usually a person's whole life), and the collateral consequences of a criminal record.

The next stage of the installation was a fortune parlor, where guests brainstormed their wildest dreams for young people and for the whole of New York City. The guests produced cards detailing their creative visions that they took to a "fortune inker"—a YNY graduate—who came up with a word to represent that guest with their fortune fulfilled and used eyeliner to "tattoo" that word on their body. Each card was tied to a hydrangea (a flower chosen by graduates because they resemble brains). As the guests left the courtroom installation, they received hydrangeas with another person's vision for New York City and its court-involved young adults.

Wisdom Gift Exchange
Eastern District Court
New York, New York, fall 2017

Wisdom Gift Exchange was created by a group of young women in a RAD program. The work celebrated giving young adults a chance to learn from their mistakes and meditated on the wisdom that can be gained when teens and young people are given a chance to grow rather than subjected to punitive sanctions. Participants transformed the courtroom by lining the benches with aspirational self-portraits, floating a silver curtain cube made from 200 silver helium balloons in front of the judge's bench, and creating interactive posts, or Wisdom Creation Stations, that encouraged criminal legal professionals to connect with YNY participants.

At the first Wisdom Creation Station, guests jotted on shiny Wisdom Disks an insight they had gleaned from a past mistake. After presenting their disks to a YNY graduate stationed in the witness stand, guests were certified "wise" and presented with a Wisdom Certification Medallion.

At another station, attendees decorated the medallions with silver boxes, bows, and gems. YNY participants also photographed the guests atop the Wisdom Throne—the judge's bench—with their Wisdom Gifts. Finally, as they departed, guests exchanged their own Wisdom Gifts for those created by other attendees, sharing wisdom and insight among members of the YNY community.

opposite, top: Floating silver curtain cube at Eastern District Court

opposite, bottom: Eastern District courtroom before arrival of guests
Photos: Mansura Khanam

top: YNY graduate
Emmanuel certifying
a guest "wise"

bottom, right: YNY
graduate and exhibition
attendee writing on
Wisdom Disks

opposite: YNY
graduate wrapping
Wisdom Gifts

Photos: Mansura Khanam

bottom, left: Guest
filling out Wisdom Disk

Artist Advocates
Eastern District Court
New York, New York, spring 2016

This eight-week RAD program focused on the idea of advocates and advocacy. Who are advocates in criminal cases? Who are advocates in the courtroom? How can people advocate for themselves? And how can YNY participants advocate for criminal legal reform?

Young people in the program designed an art game that reimagined the criminal legal system as a gold-spangled labyrinth. Guests—judges and assistant district attorneys involved with the participants' cases—played the game by moving through a series of steps as if they themselves had been arrested:

1. Enter the criminal justice system when you are 16 years old.
Guests chose a card detailing the case of a YNY participant, all of whom were arrested and charged as adults at 16 or 17 years old.

2. Make your story bigger than your case.
Attendees collaged images to create masks that represented who they were beyond their arrest, exemplified their strengths, and symbolized their future goals.

3. Advocate for yourself.
Guests thought back on their lives at 16 years old and wrote down the advice they would have given themselves on how to advocate for themselves. These kernels of advice were attached to golden hats, brooches, and flags.

4. Appear before the judge's bench.
Attendees were photographed in front of a gold-draped judge's bench.

By envisioning themselves as passing through the labyrinth of the criminal legal system, the guests gained insight on how those in the system—court professionals and young people alike—can advocate for themselves or others.

top: YNY graduate/peer mentor Shawnti guarding the labyrinth exit as a guest poses in front of the judge's bench

bottom: YNY graduate Monasia draping a sequined shawl over a masked guest

Photos: Sina Basila Hickey

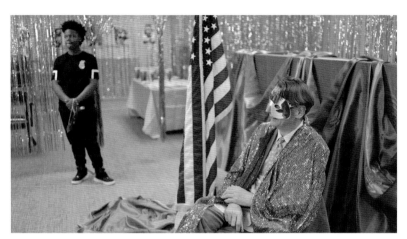

opposite: Judge Joseph E. Gubbay with YNY's Shawnti
Photo: Coke O'Neal

top: Guest with mask and props
Photo: Sina Basila Hickey

bottom, left: Assistant District Attorney Shakiva Pierre in front of the judge's bench
Photo: Coke O'Neal

bottom, right: Guest wearing hat with a memory of life at 16 years old
Photo: Sina Basila Hickey

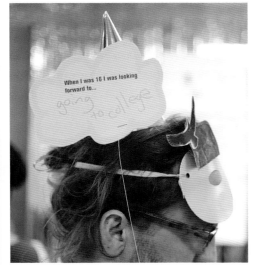

Wisdom Pavilion
NYC Public Artist in Residence at the Department of Probation
Brooklyn, New York, ongoing

In 2018, the commissioner of the NYC Department of Probation put out a call for an artist in residence. The artist would use art as a tool to improve relationships between probation officers and clients. The ultimate goal was to improve case outcomes, that is, having more clients successfully finish their terms of probation. This aspiration aligns with YNY's goal of ending mass incarceration and keeping the communities of New York City whole.

Rachel G. Barnard, founder of YNY, was named the artist in residence. Along with several probation officers, she developed *Wisdom Pavilion*, a fantastical structure made of pinwheels inside the heavily surveilled waiting room at the DOP in Brooklyn. Barnard or a trained "art listener" led listening sessions with probation officers and clients within the immersive installation.

The sessions recenter the voices of those who are most impacted by the criminal legal system; develop insights into the cultural and structural barriers faced by clients; and strengthen relationships, communication, and engagement between probation officers and the people under their supervision. *Wisdom Pavilion* uses design to create opportunities for reconfiguring interpersonal connections in a positive way and to promote a shared sense of belonging. Ultimately, the goal is to have more clients avoid jail or prison and remain in their communities.

Supported by A Blade of Grass Fellowship

opposite, top: First *Wisdom Pavilion* design rendered by collaborator Rebecca Lorenz

opposite, bottom: Supplies for pinwheel-making party

below: *Wisdom Pavilion*
installed in Department
of Probation waiting room
Photo: Mansura Khanam

top, left: YNY graduate assembling pinwheel

top, right: Rachel G. Barnard in listening session with Department of Probation Commissioner Ana Bermudez

bottom: Rachel G. Barnard in listening session with YNY graduate Monica

Photos: Mansura Khanam

Jennifer Bonner

MALL

46 *Domestic Hats*
50 *Yard Art*
52 *The Dollhaus*
56 *Glittery Faux-Facade*
60 Haus Gables
66 MISC

It's all ordinary stuff: gable roofs, hipped roofs, shed roofs, picture windows, yard art, synthetic stucco, faux-brick, reflective roadway paint, BLTs, grilled cheese, sub sandwiches, CMU block, scalloped shingles, vinyl siding, artificial turf. And the list goes on.

If Robert Venturi and Denise Scott Brown grappled with "nonstraightforward architecture," arguing for the messy over the obvious, the ambiguous over the articulated, and the hybrid over the pure, and Aldo Rossi tackled "nameless architecture," MALL expands on ideas of the ordinary. Vying for everyday errors rather than architectural correctness and casual form rather than overly coordinated geometry, the project of ordinary architecture finds a foothold in the "contractor canon" and not in close readings of prestigious precedents. That is to say, studying the roof construction of a contractor spec house is a first step in advancing the architectural imagination from what might be considered unassuming material to a generative project.

The ordinary is often overlooked. It represents the immediately accessible, which is typically tossed aside as not "architectural" enough. Overly familiar, the ordinary is basic, yet it is also fundamental to many problems in architectural discourse today. The future of the ordinary is a continuation of what is already known, but at the same time, it presents an opportunity to fuse the imagination and contemporary culture into a larger architectural project, one that may be realized in novel forms, alternatives for public space, and unprecedented representation.

In the practice, each project on the ordinary begins with a self-initiated conceptual agenda situated and sheltered by academia. Over time, easily several years, the abstract creative work evolves into something that can be represented in various media—writing, lectures, and exhibitions—and finally develops a robust footing. At this point, MALL seeks avenues for realizing the work into fully built structures.

Domestic Hats
AIA/YAF Emerging Voices Exhibition, Goats Farm Arts Center
Atlanta, Georgia, 2014

Domestic Hats uses ordinary roof typologies to reconsider the role of the massing model in architectural representation. A short drive around Atlanta demonstrates myriad stylistic differences in domestic architecture. In MALL's project, the single most effective architectural element in understanding these differences is the roof. More complex and elaborate rooflines are found in more affluent neighborhoods; simple single-gable and hipped roofs top houses in lower-income areas. MALL is interested in both.

Massing models are usually small, the result of a quick, iterative design process. They represent a schema, a diagram, a proto-architecture. When roof forms are rendered in white, the aesthetic of "home" is absent. Abstraction allows banal volumes and weirdly proportioned masses to be read as advantageous. Lacking detail and often made out of a single material, massing models allow for a cute collection of volumes—"slightly thinner," "no, a little longer," or better yet, "let's make it fatter."

Domestic Hats rejects the constraint of smallness and scales the models up to an awkward size. They don't quite fit into the frame of our foam wire cutter, nor are they easily transportable, nor do they sit comfortably on a client's conference table. These massing models do not stand in for something else; instead, they represent themselves and reveal new "hats" for consideration in domestic architecture. One of the massing models from *Domestic Hats* was eventually translated into a built work, Haus Gables.

Project team: Ainsley McMaster, Son Vu
Fabrication team: Ishrat Lopa, Jessica Greenstein

top, left: Exhibition view
Photo: Patrick Heagney

top, right:
Massing models

bottom:
Mega-massing model
Photo: Patrick Heagney

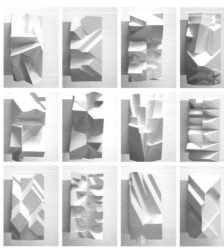

below: Exhibition view
Photo: Patrick Heagney

opposite, top:
Massing model

opposite, bottom:
Razzle-dazzle roof
surface drawings

Yard Art
Atlanta, Georgia, 2014

After the *Domestic Hats* exhibition closed, the massing models were installed in front of the houses where the original research took place; in these positions, they sat awkwardly atop grass lawns or concrete sidewalks. To suggest that scholarly architectural research can be reconfigured as kitsch garden decor is precisely the point. Stripped of all construction details—roofing material, gutters, windows, doors—*Yard Art* playfully suggests that close attention to the roof might start to alter the aesthetic of domestic architecture. Recontextualizing the models contrasts a familiar image of housing with unfamiliar architectural objects more comfortably viewed within a gallery setting.

opposite: *Yard Art No. 6* (top),
No. 7, No. 4 (middle row),
No. 2, No. 3 (bottom row),
15-by-12-inch prints
Photos: Caitlin Peterson

The Dollhaus
Chicago Architecture Biennial
Chicago, Illinois, 2017

If *Domestic Hats* questioned the role of the massing model in architectural representation, *The Dollhaus* pivots the viewer's attention toward objects of popular culture, specifically toys. Instead of the white EPS foam and abstract, monolithic roof forms of *Domestic Hats*, *The Dollhaus* reimagines the domestic interior by means of boldly patterned materials, saturated colors, and a childlike view of architecture. Additionally, the plywood model installation, which mimics a suburban house, represents ordinary architecture; humorous and idiosyncratic, the "house" calls attention to past memories and spatial relationships. There is a pluralism at work in this study: within the project's intended banality is a common language for connecting other demographics. Dollhouses are playful and relatable.

Scaled at 1:12, the universal scale for dollhouses, the model is constructed of Baltic birch plywood, card stock, and brass hardware hinges. One elevation is split in half, allowing for a doors-open view of the interior roof surfaces and rooms. MALL worked closely with food photographer Adam DeTour to light *The Dollhaus* with syrupy pink and blue lights, calling further attention to "playing house."

Project team: Benzi Rodman

opposite: Playing
house (dining and living)
Photo: Adam DeTour

Glittery Faux-Facade
Bits n' Bobs, Yve Yang Gallery
Boston, Massachusetts, 2017

Southerners have a long history of being unable to afford precious materials; instead, they have developed a knack for "faking it." *Glittery Faux-Facade* is an experiment in using faux-finishing on exterior surfaces. The installation consists of a series of stucco panels that have been molded with custom stamps to mimic bricks and wood siding. Inspired by Mary Corse's *White Light Paintings* (1968), the stucco panels are dash-finished with millions of glass beads, generating a glittery reflectivity. The glass beads, commonly used by the U.S. Department of Transportation for roadway striping, produce shimmering and glowing effects that can be applied at the scale of domestic architecture. Like *Domestic Hats, Glittery Faux-Facade* allows the discovery of ideas through architectural representation—in this case, stucco as bricks—and simultaneously connects drawing and raw material for Haus Gables.

Research assistant: Alex Timmer

opposite: Installation view
Photo courtesy Yve Yang Gallery

top: 1:1 scale panels installed at Haus Gables
Photo: NAARO

bottom: Custom tools: brick stamp, glass beads, woodgrain roller

middle: Flash photo of mock-up Photo: Anita Kan

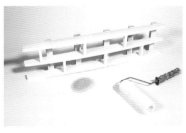

Haus Gables
Atlanta, Georgia, 2018

In an attempt to rework spatial paradigms of the past, namely Le Corbusier's free plan and Adolf Loos's *raumplan*, MALL has organized a house interior by means of the roof, aligning rooms, catwalks, and double-height spaces with its ridges and valleys. Typically, the floor plan generates the roof plan; in this case, the opposite is true.

The resulting 2,200-square-foot single-family residence in Atlanta was at the time of completion one of a handful of houses in the United States built entirely with cross-laminated timber, an innovative engineered wood. From the curb, Haus Gables appears as an asymmetrical form, as if the configuration of a traditional gable-roof house was clipped. Six gables are cut into the four facades of the house, giving rise to various strange profiles. Exterior and interior walls, floors, and roof are made of solid cross-laminated timber. Unlike stick-frame construction, custom-cut CLT panels, which can be hoisted into place and assembled in fourteen days' time, create a solid, thermally sound structure. In collaboration with multiple engineers, MALL developed the inventive roof composition as a folded plate. With no need to treat the surface, this structural material also provides the primary interior finish.

Additionally, the residence engages in a conceptual exploration of materiality. Faux-finishes on exterior and interior surfaces include thin black terrazzo tiles rather than poured in place, ceramic tiles that imitate oriented strand board, wall covering made of vinyl that emulates wood flooring, and bathroom tiles with a cartoonish drawing of Italian marble. With its unconventional materials and unusual roof plan, Haus Gables explores the function of form, spatial organization, and innovation in domestic architecture.

Project team: Ben Halpern, Benzi Rodman, Justin Jiang, Dohyun Lee, Daniela Leon
CLT manufacturer: KLH USA
CLT installation specialist: Terry Ducatt
Structural engineers: AKT II, Bensonwood, PEC Structural, Fire Tower
Associate architect: Olinger Architects
Landscape design: Carley Rickles
Mechanical systems: Emily McGlohn

top: Kitchen

bottom, right: Bedroom
Photos: NAARO

bottom, left: Upstairs
landing; bedroom
nested in larger roof

opposite, top: Haus
Gables in neighborhood
context Photo: Tim Hursley

opposite, bottom left:
West facade/street view
Photo: NAARO

opposite, bottom right:
Plans, levels 1 and 2

below: Section with
faux-finishes

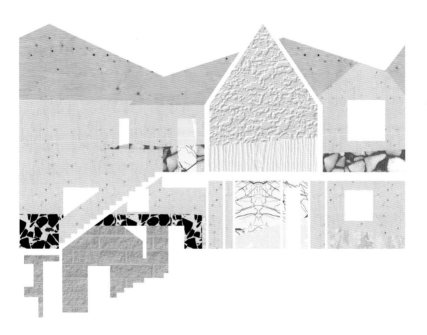

MISC
Research and installation projects
2016–2019

Odds and ends, marginalia, ideas for architecture: MALL undertakes a wide range of creative pursuits. Not all of this work fits neatly into a portfolio or single theme, but it reveals how the practice creates conceptual material. A grab bag of ideas, MISC is unconnected to the traditions of architectural practice; as is MALL's custom, the research will inform the built work in years to come.

A project for Boston's Greenway, *Another Axon*, begins with an axonometric—the architect's trusty drawing—and blends a material obsession (synthetic stucco dyed indigo blue) with cultural norms (wedding photography). *Best Sandwiches* delves into popular culture's fixation on "the best" by identifying sandwiches connected to city-based proclamations: "LA's best pastrami sandwich," "Philly's best cheesesteak," and so on. The result: a collection of nine colorful sandwiches first rendered as a picnic still life and later developed into *Office Stack*, a speculative midrise office tower.

Other projects such as *Platform: Still Life* benefit from ideas found in art practice, inspiring a book and exhibition designed for the Harvard Graduate School of Design, where 17 still lifes connect hundreds of student models across four disciplinary programs. *Haus Scallop, Haus Sawtooth* stages a performance at Mies van der Rohe's famed Haus Lange and Haus Esters in Krefeld, Germany. Two drones work in synchronization to scan the rear facades brick coursing by brick coursing. MISC represents an ongoing, never-ending stream of inspiration for architecture.

opposite (clockwise from top left): *Still Life* exhibition, Haus Lange/Haus Esters performance, faux Mies material renderings

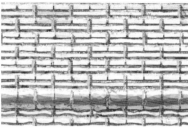

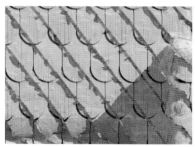

opposite: *Another Axon,*
Best Sandwiches

below: *Best Sandwiches,*
Office Stack

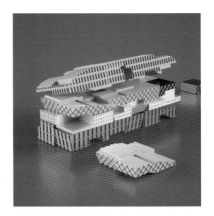

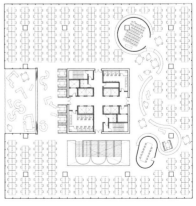

Virginia Black, Rosana Elkhatib, and Gabrielle Printz

feminist architecture collaborative

72 *Cosmo-Clinical Interiors of Beirut*
76 *Post-Fordist Hymen Factory*
80 *Still I Rise: Gender, Feminisms, Resistance*
84 *#icalled*
88 *Republic of Body*
92 *Representative Bodies*
94 *WMNs Work*

feminist architecture collaborative practices through both architecture and its refusal. Given the problematic state of practice—the crises internal to precarious architectural work and those that lie beyond the scope of righteous architectural "solutions"—we find it necessary to disavow the very frame through which we, as architects, act in the world. So we search for the exit points and edges of a fraught discipline: opportunities to deny the structural confines of the canon, historically built by men and capital; to exploit its rifts; to appropriate and export its discourses, techniques, and resources. At these edges, we also seek opportunities to usher in matter presumed to sit beyond architecture's disciplinary concerns. What other interests might be served by spatial thinking and making?

"Justice," as an object of design, has not typically referred to the project of *making just* but rather to the business of producing architectural enclosures that criminalize (as in the euphemistic "criminal justice center"). Architects continue to build on terms that pay only lip service to equity. With attention to these discontinuities in design and meaning, we conjoin the rhetorical and the material in the projects we take on—projects whose subjects are the teenager, the *achimama*, the border clinician, the hymen simulator, the workplace leaker, our girl Salome, and *bints* all around.[1] Our practice takes shape in some ways as advocacy but also in forms that attempt to dispel reductive interpretations of "fEmALE aRchITEct," COLLABxORATION, or ~political work~—descriptions that capitalize on the appearance of wokeness. Feminist architecture, collaborative work, and political practice are often taken to be self-evident models but are less often interrogated as the active and unstable positions that we must take between the world as it is and as it might be.

We do not see collaboration and representation as ends in themselves. Instead, we negotiate complex positions in the labor and content of our practice, which we consider a project of cultivating relationships, building mutual support, and crafting environments that repair and restore. Justness is to be found in the fiercest assertions of care, and our responsibility as architects, even if we claim the title with caution and extend it to others with reckless abandon, is to fashion circumstances that do not yet exist—for us, for her, for them. Our feminist practice was born in its absence; it was a way to confront compromising and inequitable conditions together. Queer demonstrations in Arab public space, Trumpian scenographies for protest, luxury clinics for virginal restoration, exhibitions of resistance movements past: these concerns are as much architectural as they are political.

1. *Achimama* is the Kichwa word for "midwife." *Bint* is the Arabic term for "girl" and can be wielded with affection, dismissal, or contempt.

Cosmo-Clinical Interiors of Beirut
Vi Per Gallery, Prague, Czech Republic, 2018–2019

Virginity has been, and is still, consequential to the agency, empowerment, and self-possession of women around the world. The concept of virginity—available in new commodity forms—is constructed not just at the site of the body but also in multiscale architectural operations, in the spaces that mediate between subjects and their desires. The plastic surgery clinic is a site of bodily reinvention and production. Interior finishes, collateral objects, and aesthetic protocols aid in the spatial and cultural production of contemporary virginity and sexuality. Beirut in particular—a Middle East capital for medical tourism, Arab soap-star beauty, and lingering gender and sexual norms—is a site where bodily indulgences and corrections converge in the clinic.

Cosmo-Clinical Interiors of Beirut is a physical reproduction and VR navigation of clinic interiors documented during our fieldwork in the city and acts as both record of and speculation about hymenoplastic architecture. The exhibition examines the constructed space, interior finishes, and designed protocols of the plastic surgery clinic to make perceptible its role in shaping subjects, virginity culture, and an ideal body. Architecture is understood as the confluence of the technological, social, and economic—not a built fact but an organizing force in a constellation of produced and productive objects.

VR specialist: Kathy Yuen

opposite, top:
Metaclinic map: assemblage of existing interiors remodeled and reproduced as virtual spaces

opposite, bottom:
Perfumed Lobby (imaged waiting room where patients are greeted with a scent to simulate an atmosphere of womanliness)

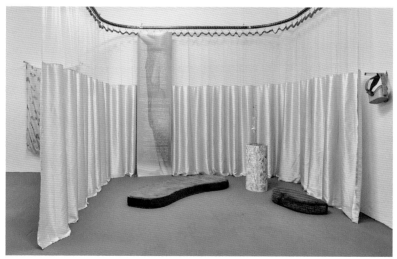

below: Perfumed
Lobby with exhibition-
goer in VR headset

opposite, top:
Sheet—a rug, a blood-
patterned plastic
membrane—laid out
to be ruined in
the Classical Suite

opposite, bottom:
Clinic rooms "worn"
through a VR headset

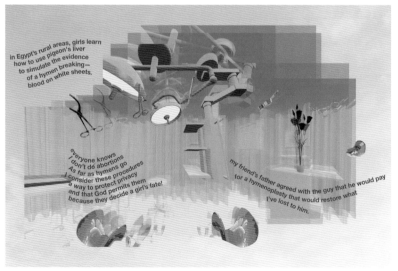

In Egypt's rural areas, girls learn how to use pigeon's liver to simulate the evidence of a hymen breaking— blood on white sheets.

everyone knows I don't do abortions As far as hymens go I consider these procedures a way to protect privacy and that God permits them because they decide a girl's fate!

my friend's father agreed with the guy that he would pay for a hymenoplasty that would restore what I've lost to him.

Virginia Black, Rosana Elkhatib, and Gabrielle Printz **75**

Post-Fordist Hymen Factory
New York, New York
2016–2017

The artificial hymen is a prosthetic artifact that circulates in markets catering to persistent notions of virginity. *Post-Fordist Hymen Factory* began as a research project to map the appearance of this synthetic bodily commodity from its site of manufacture (often China) to its points of distribution (typically Europe) and finally to its intended consumers (primarily women in the Middle East). With sensitivity to those seeking hymen simulations, but critical attention to what cultivates the need for such a product, this project intervenes in the design of the new hymen and the market in which it is made to circulate. We set out to prototype critical hymen objects—counterfeits of a counterfeited body part that elicit new performances of a performative artifact—as well as their delivery assets (packaging, instructions, and accessories) and environments of sale. A hymen with alternative forms and functions both disrupts and recirculates notions of virginity in the spaces where it is commodified, heightening the performative nature of "virginity for sale."

The intervention becomes public by its reintroduction back into market spaces. The associated e-commerce environments and temporary retail pop-ups are digital and architectural extensions of the critically rebranded hymen. Resituated within such environments of exchange, virginity prostheses assume greater scales, more explicit relationships to architecture, and a visibility that avoids placing undue pressure on the bodies of Arab women. In formulating new visual and spatial interfaces in which the hymen is simulated, we expand the possibilities of plasticity for this little seen but acutely consequential part of the body. But by negotiating virginity as, primarily, an object of design, we also challenge the moral and regulatory frameworks that act in gendered ways and to the disadvantage of subjects whose social value remains tethered to stable forms of whole and intrinsic "femaleness."

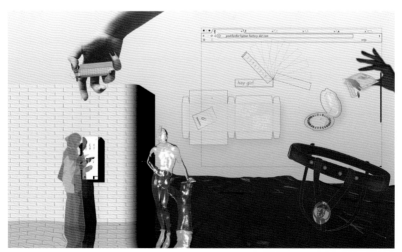

Virginia Black, Rosana Elkhatib, and Gabrielle Printz **77**

a blood stained sheet
the evidence of virginity taken—blood
on white (marital) sheets—has been
simulated for centuries, and continues
to be performed, with blood from
pigeons, sheep, and self-inflicted
wounds to attest to this valued loss. The
expectation of blood on bedsheets still
lingers in the cultures of virginity across the
world, even those that have disbanded with the value
of virginity itself. This image from Women's Health
Magazine reinforces the public conciousness of virginity
by way of the bloody sheet

**a formal virginity document and
the commitment covenant**
certain documents are signed by a young woman and
witnessed by a figural father—her parent or her
pastor—to guarantee sexual abstinence. The papers
secure a state of virginity as a ritual act but testify to that
virginity in the documentary form. A similar contract
attests to the purity of consecrated virgins in the Catholic
church: nuns, who by oath maintain a non-sexual
relationship with Jesus Christ

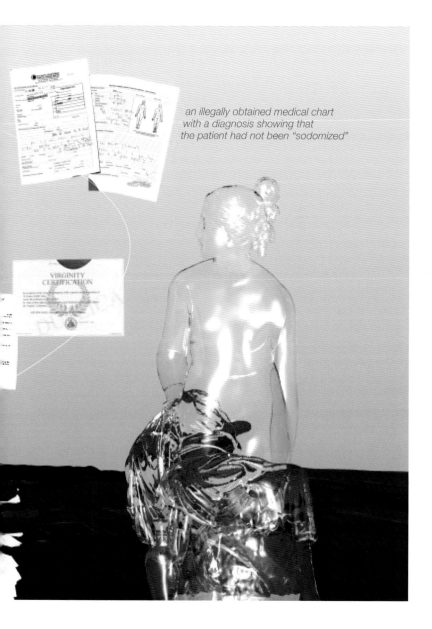

an illegally obtained medical chart
with a diagnosis showing that
the patient had not been "sodomized"

VIRGINITY
CERTIFICATION

Still I Rise: Gender, Feminisms, Resistance
In collaboration with Irene Aristizábal, Rosie Cooper, and Cédric Fauq
Nottingham Contemporary, Nottingham, England, 2018–2019
De La Warr Pavilion, Bexhill-on-Sea, England, 2019

The exhibition *Still I Rise* situates feminism and queerness as the energies behind a long and multivalent history of protest and the cultivation of alternative forms of living. Dispensing with fixed chronologies and static identities, the project assembles thematic moments of resistance from around the world: intimate acts to large-scale uprisings, late nineteenth century to the present and beyond.

Freestanding walls, niches, and furniture scaled to both the body and the crowd form the exhibition infrastructure. These composite assemblies provide variable atmospheres and mounting strategies for a diverse set of materials: stretched fabric, for instance, assumes the inner and outer faces of a curved wall and provides a tactile surface for viewing and touching. Detailing across the soft surfaces that clothe steel frames evidences the labor of the body; this kind of work, of stitching together, is visible elsewhere in the exhibition—in banners and other textile pieces. "Curtain walls" undulate to provide an open interiority but lend stature and solidity where needed. Plywood surfaces with expressed edges are also hung and wrap over the top of the wall framing. Steel frames recur throughout the exhibition in multiple permutations: in a substantial wall structure, in legs for ribbonlike tables, in the armature for the stretched-fabric niche. Somewhere between the living room and the street, the gallery opens another forum for the continued discourse of resistance.

top: View of installation from sidewalk

bottom: Four zones of exhibition: action, declaration, broadcast, reproduction

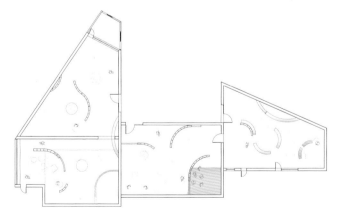

top: Living room scenography coupling activity on the street with televised images of protest

bottom: Table of archival materials connecting two galleries

top: Works by Judy Chicago, Margaret Harrison, and Feminist Land Art Retreat in area on environment, land claims, and the commons

bottom: Suffragette banners, print ephemera, and zine library in area on protest media

#icalled
Forward Union Fair; The New School; Morgan Library and Museum
New York, New York, 2016–2017

#icalled is a deployable installation and media apparatus to scene new performances of political speech. An Instagrammable call to arms, this multimedia scenography empowers citizens (and those to whom the privilege of the vote is denied) to voice resistance in three forums simultaneously: in direct calls to elected officials, in videos posted to social media, and in spectacles on the street.

This vehicle for resistance was prepared in the wake of the 2016 election, as the plurality of Americans who did not vote for Trump reacted to the reality of his presidency. In an effort to secure the White House–cum–penthouse within the domain and interests of the public, we appropriated the idiosyncratic finishes of Trump-branded residences as the businessman prepared to renovate the highest office in the land. With the material that decorated his claim to power and wealth, we employed Trumpian interior design to host other political speech: gilded props riffed on the chintzy Versailles decoration of his New York apartment, and a printed wallpaper photo backdrop incorporated his own self-tanned visage. In doing so, we proposed that the power of aesthetics—in addition to the power of space and occupation—might exert discourses overlooked by legislators and the executive.

A hashtagged video message to a specific elected official is both the product and the record of this installation, a new entry in the emerging genre of political selfies. *#icalled* exploits the minimal political cachet of the #ivoted selfie to examine how the less glamorous and non-ritual activities of political participation inhabit the aesthetic lexicon of performative social media.

Rarely is protest afforded an interior beyond those it claims for itself (the sit-in, the space forged by bodies in alliance on the street). *#icalled* establishes a public and mobile inside for hosting political dissent against powers historically formalized by architecture.

opposite, top:
#icalled implementing a performative mode of contemporary political participation

opposite, bottom:
Wallpaper with details from Trump's New York penthouse, unnatural blonde hair, and fake tan

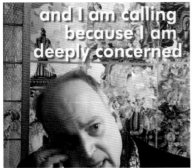

and I am calling because I am deeply concerned

and I am really concerned with the recent appointees to the new presidency's cabinet

—to commit to protecting women's reproductive rights and freedoms.

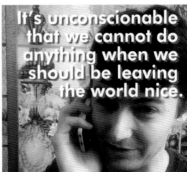

It's unconscionable that we cannot do anything when we should be leaving the world nice.

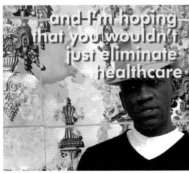

and I'm hoping that you wouldn't just eliminate healthcare

Please block his appointment.

Republic of Body
Amman, Jordan, 2016

Republic of Body is a march, part ritual procession and part gay pride parade, that stakes a claim to the streets of Amman. This *Republic* is a nation constructed of and by precarious sexual bodies. In an assertion of spatial sovereignty, otherwise denied to them as queer and femme users of public space, the bodies of *Republic* appropriate Hashemite nation-building narratives and symbols of power—symbols that themselves were borrowed from the colonial residue of the British mandate. The march occasioned new performances, costumed with the multisymbolic objects of this layered history, to disrupt a gendered national inheritance. By reproducing these mimetic symbols, the members of *Republic* express the intersection and mutual construction of queer, Arab, and gender identities and assert their right to space and legitimacy under the persistently masculine hegemony over the public sphere.

Modeled after Hashemite royal processions, *Republic of Body* was ritualized as an extension of royal ceremonies, conferring the power of an official appearance to bodies otherwise marginalized in gendered public space. The march, conducted on Al-Shari'a Street, required a complex permitting process—a separate parade, this one through municipal government. Only through this bureaucratic labor did the police come to lead our motorcade of bodily armatures (another protective measure) carrying local feminist and queer artists. Guarded by the very state that delegitimizes them, the performers assumed visible orientations on the street: a queer body veiled and externalized by an accusatory soundbite; a materialization of the elusive modern Arab woman, who otherwise exists only on virtual stages; a Jordanian scarf made to take on a femininity that it denies.

Artists: Fadi Zumot, Mohammad Tayyeb, Shireen Talhouni, Dima Hourani

top: Reappropriating
the helmet of the
Jordanian National
Guard, a sovereign
symbol at the scale
of the body

bottom: Shari'a
Street: site of the
final performance

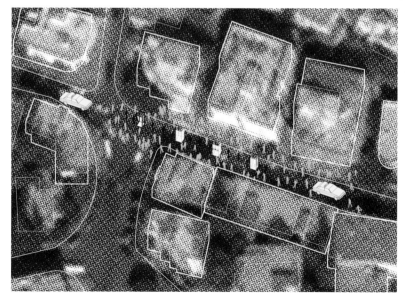

below: Space for
feminist and queer
artists instantiated
by march

top: Mohammad Tayyeb, sounds and bodily movements that subvert the space of Arab hetero-masculinity

middle: Sweet, "feminine" hibiscus tea reimagined as unrefined sour juice that invites its drinkers to join the (in)dependence (performed by Sami Nada)

bottom: Shireen Talhouni, materialization of the modern Arab woman within the physical drama of the street

Representative Bodies
In collaboration with AMUPAKIN
UN-Habitat III Conference
Quito, Ecuador, 2016

Representative Bodies presences the women of AMUPAKIN (Asociación de Mujeres Kichwas Parteras del Napo) on an international, diplomatic stage. With the group's Amazonian Kichwa midwives as collaborators, we designed official appearances across multiple formats: an act of peaceful protest, a publication, a conversation and act of live drawing, and a space of economic exchange. All of these efforts asserted an image of an Indigenous, feminine, rural identity at the UN-Habitat III Conference in Quito.

The conference, convened to focus on the implementation of the New Urban Agenda, professed to include minority voices (including Indigenous and women actors) within the space of the city. However, while the agenda makes commitments to explore the power of the city as a sustainable entity, it does not question the city as something that engenders, among other things, the destruction of other habitats it depends on for survival. In the associated processes of extraction, logging, burning, and colonizing territories, city creation also isolates the ways of thinking and being of those who live in the affected territories.

Our design intent in each facet of the project was to give presence to a concept of life and development the UN has overlooked: in this case, the inhabitation and design of the rainforest, which is an autonomy-generating practice. Within and around the space of the conference, each appearance showcased AMUPAKIN's knowledge of Indigenous birthing, healing, and cultivation practices undertaken in the Amazonian rainforest for centuries.

opposite: Publication displayed at Arte Actual's *Mapear no es Habitar* exhibition

top: Occupation by f-architecture and the *achimamas*, or midwives, of AMUPAKIN

bottom: *Achimamas* performing cleansing rituals on conference participants

WMNs Work
Archidona, Ecuador, 2016

WMNs Work is a proposal conceived to maintain our collaboration with AMUPAKIN and devise sensitive but desperately needed infrastructure to support the group's existing cultural center. To that end, this project sets out to design and construct a community-powered wireless internet system (a WMN, or Wireless Mesh Network) along the Amazon River.

Money from the global oil economy, which amounts to 42 percent of Ecuador's GDP, circulates in a network out of reach of Indigenous communities in Amazonian Ecuador. Many Kichwa people can barely afford to travel to the city via bus to sell their agricultural products. Conversely, they use canoes to travel down the river at a slower pace and a cheaper rate. Internet and other communications networks are rarely accessible. Instead, the telecom infrastructure coincides with the roads associated with petroleum transport and the larger economy of extraction.

With this proposal, AMUPAKIN, already steward of cultural practices in Amazonian Ecuador, takes responsibility for local internet. The mesh network, installed in relation to water travel networks, services Indigenous economies and their political voices, becoming a truly integral part of their existing practices of communication and exchange. To that end, the project engages an understanding of the way in which the internet, as a material object, can be constructed, monumentalized, and distributed to cater to a variety of community spatial practices.

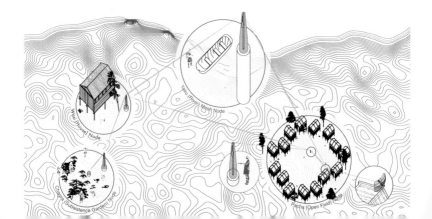

opposite: Mesh
network diagram

below: Research on the
design and prototyping
of constituent nodes
in a dispersed wireless
internet system

centralized network

access node system

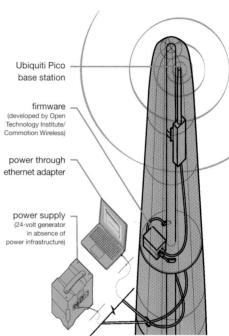

Ubiquiti Pico
base station

firmware
(developed by Open
Technology Institute/
Commotion Wireless)

power through
ethernet adapter

power supply
(24-volt generator
in absence of
power infrastructure)

open mesh network:
global internet connection

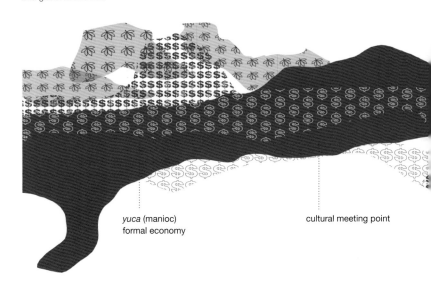

yuca (manioc)
formal economy

cultural meeting point

petroleum transport route

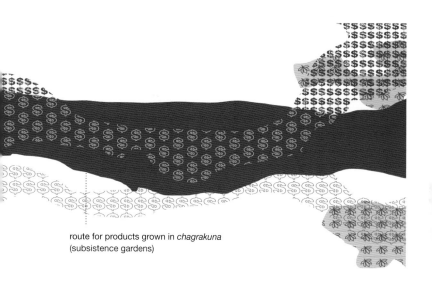

route for products grown in *chagrakuna*
(subsistence gardens)

ower

oil drilling area

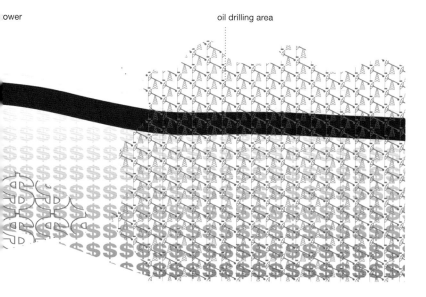

Mira Hasson Henry

(HA)

100   *Rough Coat*

104   Silver House Studio

108   *Not White Walls*

112   *Not White Walls (Postscript)*

116   *The View Inside*

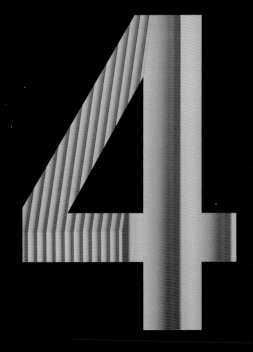

In the late 50s Ad Reinhardt famously declared he was "making the last paintings that could be painted." Now, what am I supposed to do with that, given, on the one hand, how marginal Black figure images are in the archive of art history, and on the other, the absence of Black artists in the ranks of the innovative avant-garde.

—Kerry James Marshall, *Who's Afraid of Red, Black and Green*

The projects I include here reflect a sense of urgency to challenge the hermetic culture of architectural formalism. This is optimistic work, based on the belief that when we structure an architectural idea, we may choose to ground it in a diverse set of critical values. Issues of formal technique, material experimentation, and representation are often comfortably seated in discrete spaces of autonomy. I am interested in crosscutting and interrupting these concerns with what I describe as particular conditions of the present. These conditions reflect the quotidian circumstances around any project: its context, who makes it, how it is made, and the way it is publicly consumed. Through this confrontation, formal ideation is implicitly informed by and bound up in contemporary concerns of race, gender, and desire. In order to traverse autonomous formal thinking and situated political conditions, I explore tactics that privilege attention to mild absurdities, mundane details, and coincidences of association. As a result, a vague tension hovers in the background of any given project, like a gentle nudge or a cutting look. With an eye toward the just, I see these projects as engaging a critical overlap between the highly calibrated means and methods of constructing a formally nuanced architecture and an insistence on interrupting the myth of cultural neutrality latent in our discipline.

Rough Coat
SCI-Arc Gallery
Los Angeles, California, 2018

This project was guided by a formal and social agenda that calls for the creation of non-normative conditions and space. *Rough Coat* is situated as the story of constructing a building-sized blanket. Blankets are soft, submissive, and tolerant. They are inviting to use and easy to put away. By contrast, buildings are heavy and labored. In bringing these disparate material systems together, a range of effects unfolds. There are parts that behave well, parts that behave badly, and parts that act in a manner we may not quite recognize. The gallery, in this context, becomes a permissive space in which dissonant readings and experiences can overlap and cohabitate. Comfort, familiarity, and play sit alongside the rough, the unrelenting, the alien. Meanwhile, the physical space of the white-box gallery is reimagined as a supersaturated and intimate interior landscape. The walls are coated in dark brown paint, the lights are turned down, and the display area is filled with layers of rough and fluffy materials that drape and pile one on top of the other. Visitors and materials alike are encouraged to take up space and engage in formal and informal ways.

Rough Coat is not about constructing a distance that allows all things to fall into focus. This stuff wants us close.

Project team: Abeeha Abid, Tamara Birghoffer, Dutra Brown, Mateus Comparato, Andy DePew, Arthur Gueiros, Bianca Hernandez, Brendan Ho, Jaqueline Huang, Pasinee Jiemcharoeying, Heyifan Jin, Esin Karaosman, Lotta Locklund, Kendall Mann, Jonathan Ong, Allyn Viault, Malvin Wibowo, Corie Yaguchi, Yi Zhan Zhong

opposite:
Installation view

Silver House Studio
In collaboration with Matthew Au, Current Interests
Los Angeles, California, ongoing

Silver House Studio is an exploration of the thickening and exaggeration of conventional building systems. The existing building is a small art studio that is pushed up against a hillside and buried under a heavy coat of greenery. Balanced above it, on the hill, is a 1920s bungalow with silver-painted lap siding, a beautiful, unusual little house with a big pyramid roof. The art studio is designed to be equally particular. A new roof consists of hung corrugated concrete shingles that have been dyed a range of near-black tones. This new covering becomes a dark and textured foreground for the silver figure beyond. Inside the studio is a custom-manufactured insulation quilt that hangs from the structure and slips in and around the interior components. It rolls up for windows and doors and peels back for lighting and outlets. We worked from the inside out and the outside in, producing a hyper-private domain that supplies a quiet presence within the city.

Design team: Austin Anderson, Ravyn Crabtree, Andrew DePew, Cole Masuno, Sofia Alma Ramos, Tucker Van Leuwen-Hall, Neil Vasquez, Corie Yaguchi

opposite: Model views
Photos: Matthew Au

below: Full-scale mock-up
Photo: Michael Vahrenwald

opposite, top left: Model
Photo: Matthew Au

opposite, middle left:
Full-scale mock-up
at Princeton School of
Architecture Gallery
Photo: Michael Vahrenwald

opposite, top right:
Full-scale mock-up
Photo: Michael Vahrenwald

opposite, bottom:
Roof shingle detail

0 2 4   6 ft.

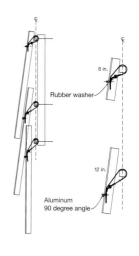

Rubber washer

Aluminum
90 degree angle

6 in.

12 in.

0 1 2 4 in.

0 1 2 4 in.

Not White Walls
Los Angeles, California, 2017–present

Upon second glance, something seems to be going on here. *Not White Walls* is about looking carefully at the vernacular conditions of single-story houses in South Los Angeles. The project emerged from a practice of moving through the city slowly and attending to the aesthetic effects associated with an acute desire for privacy. In these houses, privacy is conveyed not by mute blankness but rather through a buildup of expressive layers that together thicken the distance between exterior and interior. These layers include dramatic shrubbery, faux material cladding, high-saturation paint colors, awnings, eaves, exterior shutters, interior shutters, decorative bars, security bars, glass tinting, glass foiling, vertical blinds, horizontal blinds, and curtains of various weights and translucencies. Formally, *Not White Walls* uses manipulated images to construct a multilayered physical model that renders potent subjects that are often overlooked and underdiscussed: house accessories, landscape maintenance, practices of use, and style in Black and Brown neighborhoods in Los Angeles.

Project team: Tiziana Felice, Neil Vasquez

opposite: House survey in Los Angeles

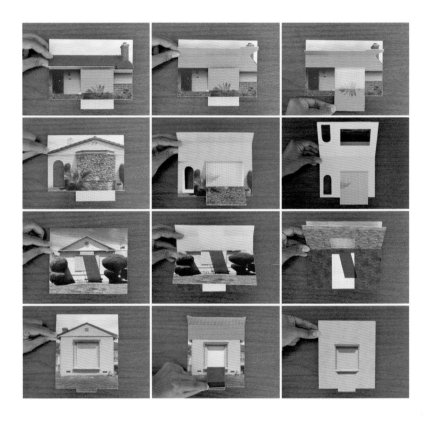

Not White Walls (Postscript)
One-Night Stand LA
Los Angeles, California, 2017

The multiplying of material layers studied in *Not White Walls* was translated into a full-scale drawing for the entry window of a hotel room provided by the *One-Night Stand* exhibition. Additionally, postcard-sized pop-up facades from the longer-term study were displayed within the room as a miniature domestic landscape.

Project team: Tiziana Felice, James Kubiniec, Neil Vasquez

opposite:
Installation view

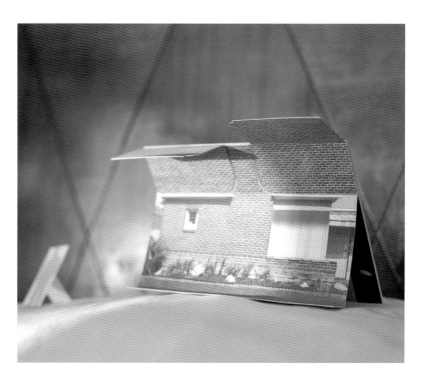

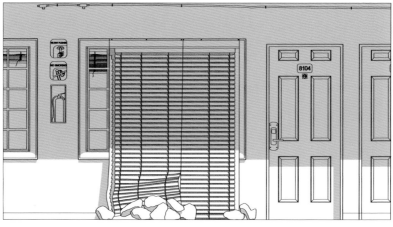

Mira Hasson Henry **115**

The View Inside
University of Michigan Museum of Art
Ann Arbor, Michigan, 2016

The View Inside explores the visual and conceptual relationship between foreground and background in a museum context. Commissioned by the University of Michigan Museum of Art, the piece began as a series of measurements and a survey of details for the gallery space. Traditionally, the museum paints its gallery walls according to what is shown: browns for the African galleries, deep purple for the South Asian rooms, maroon for the medieval wing, celadon blue for the East Asian gallery, and cool white for the modern and contemporary displays. It is as if the paint color of the walls anticipates the inhabitants. The installation re-creates an isomorphic relationship between objects and walls by means of 40 feet of wallpaper applied to the gallery. The digitally constructed wallpaper represents a room lined in color-tinted drapery that has been flattened and unfolded at a 1:1 scale. Standing in front of the wallpaper is a collection of color-matched objects and pedestals. The two-dimensional and three-dimensional materials visually commingle in quiet and persistent ways. By recasting the background, the project shifts the context of the museum toward a distant version of itself.

As presented here, photographs of the installation are accompanied by a more informal set of documents created during the production phase. Individuals of different skin tones pose in front of the wallpaper. Although the lighting conditions do not change, the color of the background shifts in a fugitive manner—from brown-gray to mauve-purple. In the images, the tools that mediate representation, such as color-balancing technology, exaggerate the relationship between bodies and space, between objects and background.

Project team: Nancy Ai, Patrick Bennett, Massimiliano Boselli, Dutra Brown, Tiziana Felice, Arthur Gueiros, Rishab Jain, Melissa Lee, Chris Nolop, Tidus Ta

opposite:
Installation view
Photo: Corine Vermeulen

top: Rendering

bottom: Model views

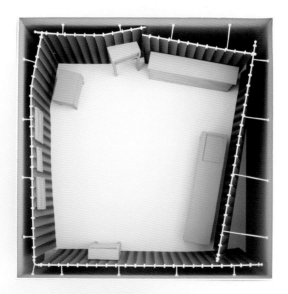

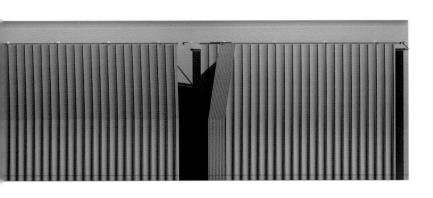

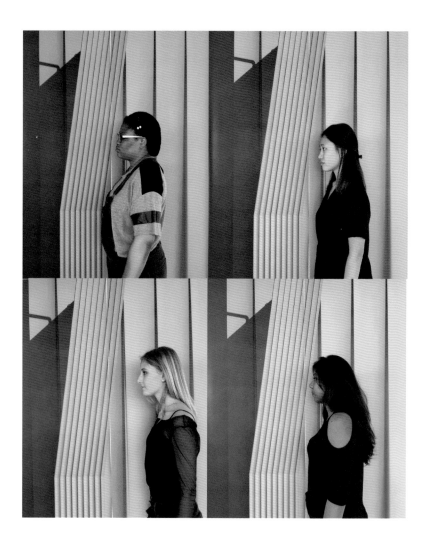

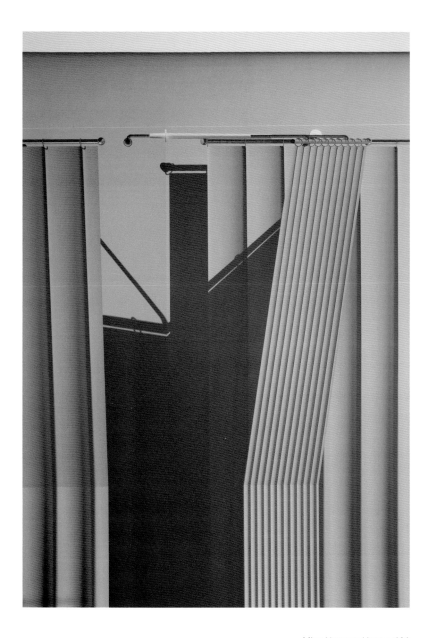

Gregory Melitonov

Taller KEN

124   Playa Chomo/FUNdaMENTAL Design-Build Initiative
130   Barrio Gerona/FUNdaMENTAL Design-Build Initiative
134   Madero Restaurant
138   Zona 14 Canopy Café
142   Fabra Facade
144   Roots School Cambodia

Over the history of the practice, Taller KEN has increasingly directed its focus to cultural relevancy and advocacy through architecture in the public realm. The work of the Latin America/New York–based office is carefully calibrated to its settings, which are often in developing countries defined by an imbalance between growth and social equity. A central premise of the studio's work is that well-founded architectural projects that represent a specific place carry the potential to critique the social concerns specific to that space.

Challenging convention and maintaining an appreciation for local expertise and tradition while operating within commercial constraints is a starting point for the studio. Beyond the faithful execution of any one project, an architect's responsibility is to use the act of building to generate dialogue around larger themes of the collective good. Principled design tied to its place is therefore vital because it engages the public, advocates for change, and creates a framework for participation, especially in areas undergoing economic transformation.

Taller KEN's body of work, rich with playful material choices, includes both commissioned commercial projects and self-initiated social projects. Consistent across the works is variation in scale and scope, attentiveness to doing more with less, research into the local landscape for know-how and inspiration, and commitment to bringing people together across social divides. As a whole, the projects demonstrate a hands-on approach to real-world opportunities as well as the resourcefulness required to work in developing, yet still underserved, regions.

Playa Chomo/FUNdaMENTAL Design-Build Initiative
Guatemala City, Guatemala, 2016

Playa Chomo, or Connection Beach, is the inaugural project of FUNdaMENTAL, an annual design-build program instituted by Taller KEN. Architecture students from around the world participate in the nonprofit initiative. The chosen structure, a permanent or temporary pavilion, is intended to generate public awareness of the conditions of the site and give rise to a process of civic and cultural renewal.

The first year, the site was at the base of the Centro Cultural Miguel Ángel Asturias, a disused theater complex in the center of Guatemala City. The team of international collaborators created a large, colorful canopy using recycled elastic ribbons. The pavilion shelters programmed events, including concerts, and resting areas. A covered gravel pathway leads from the street up to the theater grounds.

opposite, top: Design-Build Initiative team

opposite, bottom: Experiential pathway

below: Ribbon
connection

right: Installation view

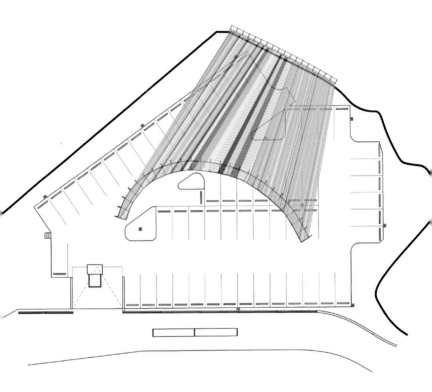

Barrio Gerona/FUNdaMENTAL Design-Build Initiative
Guatemala City, Guatemala, 2017

Taller KEN's second design-build project was located at a defunct rail depot in Barrio Gerona, an impoverished neighborhood on the fringes of Guatemala City. An urban renewal initiative, it had three distinct aspects: education of young architects and designers; planning and physical improvement of the rail corridor to benefit the district and especially the 40 families living in the adjacent housing complex; and community engagement and participation.

The designers proposed a master plan for converting the area, including informal public spaces, into a park and also set the first phase in motion. Using donated and reclaimed materials, the team created murals, landscaping, benches, and garden planters to improve the nearby housing complex.

The group established relationships with local stakeholders and residents, with the intent of providing a sense of collective ownership of the resulting installation. Neighborhood children collaborated on the murals, giving input on shapes and colors. The execution of the project brought the neighborhood together, with residents and volunteers contributing food, music, paint, brushes, and construction tools.

opposite, top:
Aerial view

opposite, bottom:
Pedestrian pathway

top: Concrete planters

bottom: Design-Build
Initiative team

opposite, top:
Rendering

opposite, bottom:
Local performers using
new public space

Gregory Melitonov **133**

Madero Restaurant

Guatemala City, Guatemala, 2015

This café and event space aims to blend the human and the industrial scale. Both exterior and interior draw inspiration from commercial roadside icons, reflecting a lighthearted yet critical approach to urban sprawl and sustainability. The exterior was conceived as a four-sided billboard at the scale of the highway. The 50-foot-tall cube studded with colorful car chassis attracts the attention of passing motorists.

The 4,500-square-foot interior is lush and highly detailed—a pastiche of technical and traditional elements. Exposed steel structure, skylights, and louvers express the building systems. Rainwater is collected in bright blue tanks and used to water the 15-foot palm trees that demarcate the open plan. The floor is a patchwork of cement tiles, some new and others recycled from local patios. These elements, combined with custom millwork, furnishings, and tropical vegetation, create a space that is at once familiar and refreshingly unexpected.

opposite, top:
Interior view

opposite, bottom:
Facade with car chassis

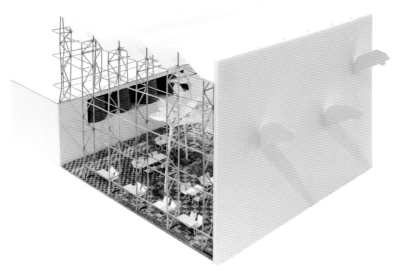

opposite, top:
Aerial view

opposite, bottom:
Diagrammatic model

top, left: Fountain

top, right: Skylights

bottom: Section

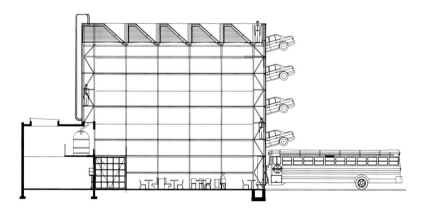

Zona 14 Canopy Café
Guatemala City, Guatemala, 2013

The light steel structure of this outdoor café supports a sunshade of nearly one thousand pounds of hand-dyed cotton yarn. The design suggests a garden pergola—in fact, the eatery is surrounded by greenery—reimagined to celebrate local expertise and tradition, in this case, the time-honored fiber crafts of the region. The yarn alludes to the dyeing process characteristic of pre-Columbian textile production. The local material used in an unconventional way; the contrasting minimal furnishings; and the texture, plantings, and natural light of the surroundings create a palpable connection to the environment and to the history of the place.

left: Yarn production in San Andrés Xecul, Guatemala

opposite, top: Interior view

opposite, bottom: Study model

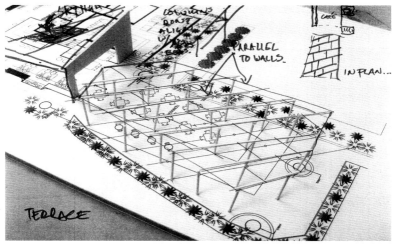

top: Plan

bottom: Study
for sunshade

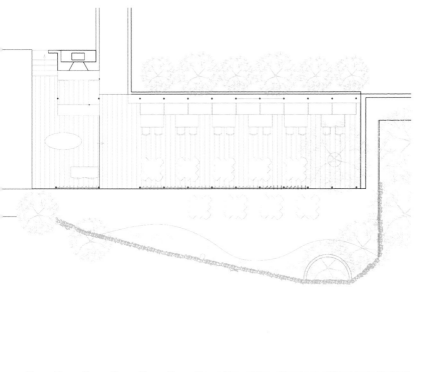

Fabra Facade
Guatemala City, Guatemala, 2017

The "site" for this facade project is a new residential building that has views of a lush, protected ravine. That ravine served as the inspiration for the "green wall" that transforms the unremarkable mid-rise structure. The new facade incorporates plant species native to the microclimate, making the building a true representation of its place.

Applied to the exterior *aleros* (concrete overhangs common to multistory buildings in the region) is a low-cost, low-maintenance green roof system. The simple "hanging gardens" on the nine upper floors create nearly two acres of green space, more than double the building's footprint. Using endemic vegetation ensures minimal watering and maintenance and creates a natural habitat for birds and other urban wildlife. Added to the building along with the soil and drainage that support the vegetation were pale blue vertical concrete panels. These elements create privacy between apartments, provide interior shade, and act as a trellis for the new vegetation.

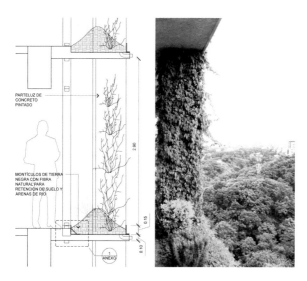

left: Section detail and photograph of typical balcony

opposite: Facade views with greenery

Roots School Cambodia
Roluos, Cambodia, ongoing

The community of Roluos in rural Cambodia is located 16 miles from the provincial capital Siem Reap and within the boundaries of the UNESCO world heritage site of Angkor. Siem Reap offers professional opportunities for educated young professionals, yet locals often lack the education to make the most of what is available. The residents of Roluos requested a specialized learning center within their village to provide their children with both life skills and instruction in English.

Roots School Cambodia consists of a series of simple pavilions. Colorful roof slopes give the pavilions a playful appearance and echo the local vernacular. Each structure contains different educational and administrative programs and may be expanded incrementally as resources become available.

top: Rendering

bottom: Cambodian
stilt houses

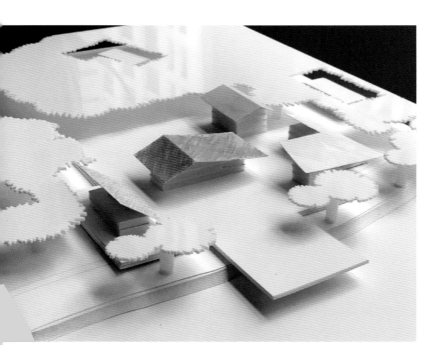

top: Section
perspective through
guest house

bottom: Section

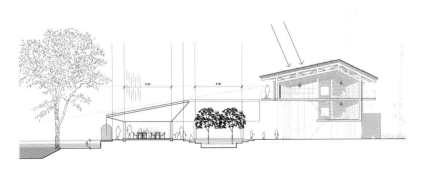

Cyrus Peñarroyo

EXTENTS

150 *Image Matters*
154 *alt+AR*
158 *Shaped Places of Carroll County New Hampshire*
164 *Other Island*
168 *Assembly Lines*
172 *Lossy/Lossless*

Some are quick to criticize architecture motivated by political activism as "just social practice," by aesthetic pursuits as "just formalism," by algorithmic control as "just parametricism," by technological misappropriation as "just post-digital," by material sensitivity as "just phenomenology," by image making as "just representation," and so on. These pronouncements reveal the breadth of our field while at the same time restricting what constitutes worthwhile work. And while some in the discipline use these reductive assessments to stifle the cultural enterprises of others, I believe that architecture can't act *justly* without engaging its limits. Instead of dismissing architecture as "not that" and "just this," EXTENTS (my partnership with McLain Clutter) turns architecture's disciplinary silos inside out. We practice architecture in a way that is extensive, not exclusive. We are fascinated by visual concerns because we believe that the aesthetic project can be political, and that politics are *always* aesthetic. We misuse the formalist palette to instigate social situations. We de-optimize algorithms to initiate novel material strategies. We manipulate digital culture to create venues for vital public engagement. We celebrate the "stuff" of appearances (screens, reflections, and texture maps) to raise questions around identity and belonging. And we exploit the soft power of images toward civic ends. In doing so, we look to renew architecture's role as a medium of collectivity and common experience for diverse, contemporary, and mediated audiences. Just have a look—in a milieu of ubiquitous imagery and snap judgments, "looking" has ethical implications.

Image Matters
Taubman College Liberty Research Annex
Ann Arbor, Michigan, 2018

If images are a ubiquitous part of our material world, what is the materiality of images? *Image Matters* explores this question through a two-part design- and making-based project. The first component is an occupiable sliding-box camera named *The Conditions Room*, a study of the spatial and material consequences of image making. The camera is clad in neoprene foam sheets, and we paid particular attention to the paneling details, which transform the light and thermal requirements for image making into architectural ornamentation. Aluminum reproductions of the details provide the substrates for the second part of the project: prototypes for a wall-panel system with embedded images. The metal pieces were photosensitized by the wet-plate collodion process, an archaic procedure involving chemical and physical reactions that produce direct-positive images. The prints—unmistakably photographic yet sufficiently distinct from most images— are meant to interrupt habitual consumption and secure rare moments of attention.

Project team: McLain Clutter, Michael Amidon, Te-Shiou Chen

opposite, top:
Wet-plate collodion
wall-panel prototype

opposite, bottom:
The Conditions Room

top: *The Conditions Room*   **bottom, left:** Wet-plate collodion wall-panel prototype   **bottom, right:** *The Conditions Room* detail

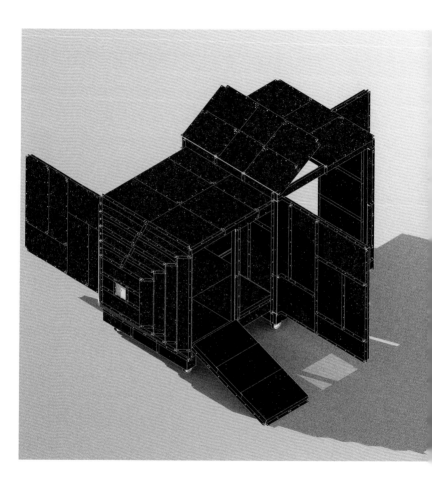

alt+AR
IRL Gallery
Cincinnati, Ohio, 2017

alt+AR is a site-specific virtual reality installation that combines a digital environment and material artifacts to produce a space of heightened attention. Using perverse forms of persuasion (mediated and sustained mimicry and levitation), the exhibition exploits everyday viewing habits and the capacity for image recognition to render the surroundings anew. Concrete units arranged in a grid orient the visitor to the room and provide the physical support for a series of metallic prints. Each print translates a mixture of religious and pop iconography into visual patterns that have virtual depth despite the fundamentally flat surface. Nested within this field of images is a VR headset. Contrary to standard practices, the device displays a version of the same gallery, producing in viewers an uncanny awareness of the surrounding space.

Project team: Chris Campbell

opposite:
Installation view

Shaped Places of Carroll County New Hampshire
Pinkcomma Gallery
Boston, Massachusetts, 2018

Shaped Places of Carroll County New Hampshire is a spatio-political satire that speculates on the reciprocity between who we are and where we live, between the identities of political subjects and the built environments that support them. The project draws on a seemingly unlikely combination of protagonists and references— from Frank Stella to early twentieth-century urbanist Mikhail Aleksandrovich Okhitovich, from American formalism to critical geography. These disparate sources, when placed into dialogue, inform the design of three linear cities in Carroll County. For some, New Hampshire's shape holds unique resonance. A notorious swing state, it remained purple on the presidential election map until late into the night of November 8, 2016. Much like the gerrymandering practices that produced those voting results, *Shaped Places* seeks to organize the population geometrically at a geographic scale in order to urbanize the rural while ruralizing the urban. Shape and content forge a complex reciprocity.

Project team: McLain Clutter, Michael Amidon, Pedro Duhart Benavides, Craig Zehr

opposite, top:
Master plans painted according to the logic of Frank Stella's *Irregular Polygons* series

opposite, bottom:
Exhibition view

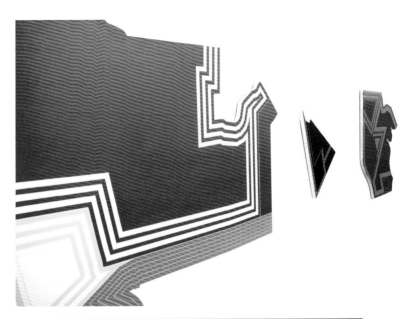

below: Sanbornville
linear city planning
unit with descriptions
based on market
segmentation tapestries

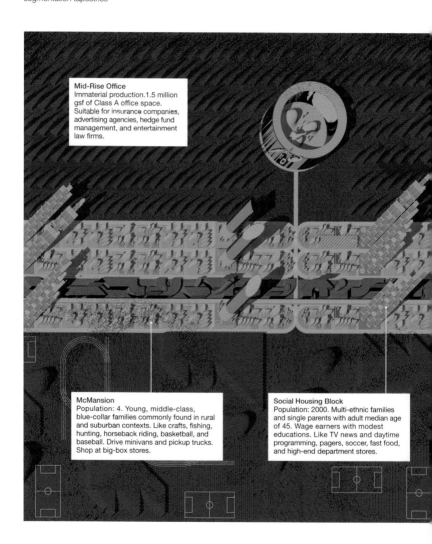

Mid-Rise Office
Immaterial production.1.5 million gsf of Class A office space. Suitable for insurance companies, advertising agencies, hedge fund management, and entertainment law firms.

McMansion
Population: 4. Young, middle-class, blue-collar families commonly found in rural and suburban contexts. Like crafts, fishing, hunting, horseback riding, basketball, and baseball. Drive minivans and pickup trucks. Shop at big-box stores.

Social Housing Block
Population: 2000. Multi-ethnic families and single parents with adult median age of 45. Wage earners with modest educations. Like TV news and daytime programming, pagers, soccer, fast food, and high-end department stores.

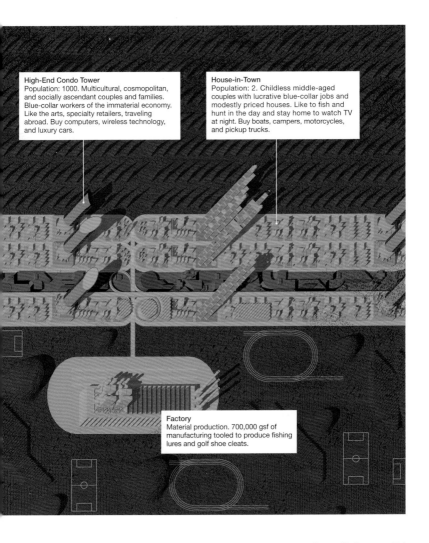

High-End Condo Tower
Population: 1000. Multicultural, cosmopolitan, and socially ascendant couples and families. Blue-collar workers of the immaterial economy. Like the arts, specialty retailers, traveling abroad. Buy computers, wireless technology, and luxury cars.

House-in-Town
Population: 2. Childless middle-aged couples with lucrative blue-collar jobs and modestly priced houses. Like to fish and hunt in the day and stay home to watch TV at night. Buy boats, campers, motorcycles, and pickup trucks.

Factory
Material production. 700,000 gsf of manufacturing tooled to produce fishing lures and golf shoe cleats.

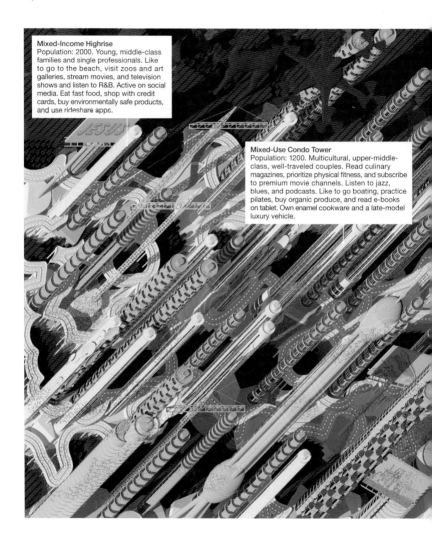

Mixed-Income Highrise
Population: 2000. Young, middle-class families and single professionals. Like to go to the beach, visit zoos and art galleries, stream movies, and television shows and listen to R&B. Active on social media. Eat fast food, shop with credit cards, buy environmentally safe products, and use rideshare apps.

Mixed-Use Condo Tower
Population: 1200. Multicultural, upper-middle-class, well-traveled couples. Read culinary magazines, prioritize physical fitness, and subscribe to premium movie channels. Listen to jazz, blues, and podcasts. Like to go boating, practice pilates, buy organic produce, and read e-books on tablet. Own enamel cookware and a late-model luxury vehicle.

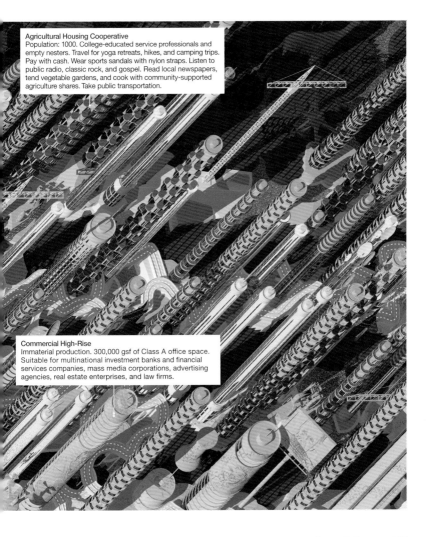

Agricultural Housing Cooperative
Population: 1000. College-educated service professionals and empty nesters. Travel for yoga retreats, hikes, and camping trips. Pay with cash. Wear sports sandals with nylon straps. Listen to public radio, classic rock, and gospel. Read local newspapers, tend vegetable gardens, and cook with community-supported agriculture shares. Take public transportation.

Commercial High-Rise
Immaterial production. 300,000 gsf of Class A office space. Suitable for multinational investment banks and financial services companies, mass media corporations, advertising agencies, real estate enterprises, and law firms.

Other Island
LA+ Imagination Competition Entry
Los Angeles, California, 2017

Other Island is an object of the imagination. From Thomas More's *Utopia* to Koolhaas and Zenghelis's New Welfare Island, islands have a long history of eliciting idealistic visions for alternative ways of life. Equal parts geographic object, optical device, and ocean liner, *Other Island* leverages this history. The vast interior, which houses the mechanical works, is occupied by an anonymous, lone operator. The exterior design is a mash-up of digital interpolations of the most enigmatic islands in the world. This crystalline massing was sculpted to create readings that oscillate between geologic and architectural forms. From some vantage points, the island seems to be a formation of rocks emerging from the sea; from other outlooks, apparent building forms come into view atop the island's iridescent chrome-plated shell. Conceptually sited within a travel itinerary, *Other Island* visits a series of the most frequently photographed global cities, reflecting and manipulating each iconic skyline on its faceted surface. The island will sometimes display visual noise or intense optical distortions; at other times, carefully orchestrated visual attenuations. Thus, strangely familiar and decisively altered images of a viewer's own city will be returned to that viewer. These playful distortions are meant to catalyze a rethinking of present-day reality by representing new ways of life, radical ecologies, and inventive material compositions.

Project team: McLain Clutter, Michael Amidon, Te-Shiou Chen

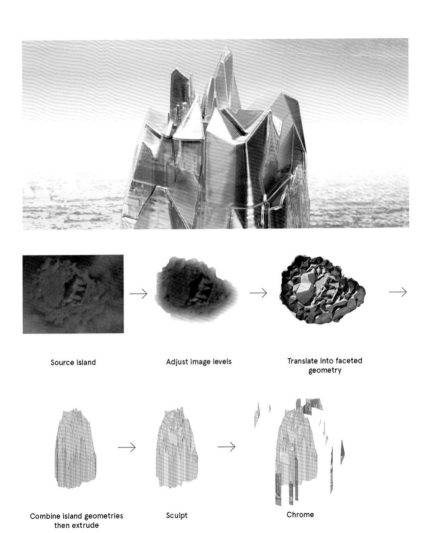

Source island

Adjust image levels

Translate into faceted geometry

Combine island geometries then extrude

Sculpt

Chrome

Assembly Lines
Design Center in a Box Competition Entry
Detroit, Michigan, 2018

What if the workers owned the factory? Detroit's industrial past saw labor tethered to the assembly line in Fordist synchrony and to the benefit of the corporation. *Assembly Lines* flips that legacy. The project is composed of a suite of graphic spatial parts, each assembled from a combination of pin-up boards, acoustic panels, and reflective surfaces. Conceived as a toolbox of elements for community use, the pieces contain everything from tables and chairs to party supplies. Mounted to casters and sliding along tracks, they can be moved to host various single-person or collective programs. The geometric relationship between the continuous linear track above and the graphic pattern on the floor suggests diverse configurations — from coworking to community design meetings. Here, lines define zones for the public to assemble and thresholds to be crossed or occupied. Adaptable and scalable, the pieces can be added or removed as local needs change. As people and parts aggregate in different ways, the space comes to resemble a factory floor, redirecting Detroit's industrial legacy toward the creative assembly of community infrastructure. Meanwhile, that community finds itself literally reflected in the mirrored surfaces of the spatial parts, branding on them a new urban image of grass-roots publics and counterpublics assembled around common concerns.

Project team: McLain Clutter, Lucas Denit

top: Public forum   **bottom:** Plan and section

below: Possible
configurations (left to right):
zone/niche, coworking/
independent working, small
discussion/large assembly

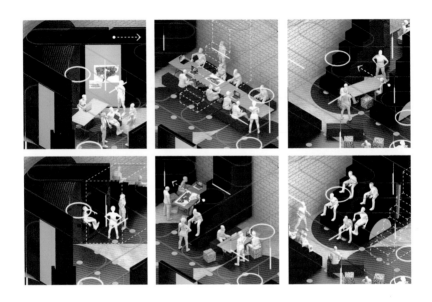

Lossy/Lossless
Materials & Applications
Los Angeles, California, 2019

Lossy/Lossless is a temporary environment for a neighborhood on the cusp of change. Located in Los Angeles in a rapidly gentrifying part of Echo Park off Sunset Boulevard, this project sought to provide a forum for discussion on the role that arts organizations play in urban development. A tableau that wraps the interior of the storefront exhibition space features asynchronous elements of the boulevard's past and future—markers of its history and signifiers of its nascent gentrification. Assembled at multiple scales to collide time and space, the tableau elements are printed on a reflective wall covering, which brings street life from the exterior into the installation. A mutable and occupiable floorscape fills the remainder of the space. Assembled using a data-center floor system, the layered platforms are covered with high-density foam padding. Various types of programming, from community meetings to after-school activities, take place on the floor; participants are reflected on the walls to become part of the changing neighborhood image.

Project team: McLain Clutter, Lucas Denit

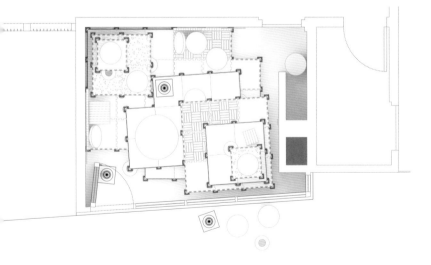

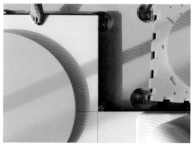

above (left to right):
Cyrus Peñarroyo,
Virginia Black, Gabrielle
Printz, Rosana Elkhatib,
Rachel G. Barnard,
Gregory Melitonov,
Jennifer Bonner, and
Mira Hasson Henry